This book is to be returned on or before the last date stamped below.

GOING LIVE! CAT BOOK

GRACE McHATTIE

BBC Books

The records for the fattest cat, the oldest cat, the largest litter of kittens, the fastest cat and the cat who travelled furthest, on pages 32 and 33, come from the *Guinness Book of Pet Records*, Guinness Publishing Ltd, copyright © Guinness Superlatives, 1984.

Published by BBC Books
a division of BBC Enterprises Ltd
Woodlands, 80 Wood Lane, London W12 OTT

First published 1990
© Grace McHattie 1990
Cartoons © Andy Cooke 1990
Diagrams © Steve Carey 1990

Reprinted 1990

ISBN 0 563 20880 5
Printed and bound by Richard Clay Limited, Bungay
Cover printed by Richard Clay Limited, Norwich

Contents

Do I really want a cat? 6
Where will I buy my kitten? 8
How do I choose a kitten? 10
What type of cat? 12
What will my new kitten need? 15
How do I keep my kitten healthy and safe? 18
What if my kitten has worms? 21
What do I feed my kitten? 23
How do I housetrain my kitten? 27
Should I let my cat have kittens? 29
Do I have to comb or brush my cat? 34
Will I ever have to bath my cat? 38
What do I do if my cat has fleas? 42
How do I know if my cat is ill? 47
Can first aid be given to an injured cat? 50
What should I do if my cat eats something poisonous? 54
Interviews 56
Like Simon, I'm allergic to cats. Is there any type of cat I can keep? 60
My cat wets on the carpets and furniture. How can I stop this? 62
Names to call your cat 66
Cats don't need any help from us when they're having kittens, do they? 74
My cat dribbles and kneads my skin with its paws when it's happy. Why? 81
I'm buying a kitten to keep my cat company. How should I introduce them? 85
Do cats like travelling? And what should I do with my cat when we move house? 90
Can I take my cat to a cat show? 93
Moggy meanings 96

Do I really want a cat?

If you've already got a feline friend, it's too late to answer that question! If you haven't think about this:

Cats live for an average 14 or 15 years. Some reach their thirties. *Will you want to look after a cat for all of its life?*

Even if your cat didn't cost you anything, over a period of 15 years it could cost as much as £5000 in food, veterinary bills, equipment and cattery fees at holiday times. *Can you afford it?*

Cats can cause damage. They may scratch the furniture or knock over an ornament by accident. *Are your parents houseproud?*

Some people are allergic to cats. *Could anyone in your household be allergic?*

Cats need to go to the toilet. They should have a litter tray for indoor use. *Who will do the poop-scooping?*

Cats like to eat – regularly. *Who will feed your cat?*

Cats are friendly and hate to be left alone all day. *Is someone at home most of the time to provide company?*

Does your family have lots of holidays or go away for weekends? *Who will look after the cat while you are away?*

And, if you particularly want to buy a kitten rather than an adult cat, remember that a kitten is:

- extremely active, naughty and can get into danger easily
- it may have a few 'accidents' before it gets the hang of its litter tray
- it will be teething and may chew everything in sight
- it won't do anything you tell it to
- it will sleep for 18 or 20 hours a day – and always when you want to play with it or show it to your friends

- it will need three or four meals a day, at regular times
- it will cost a lot of money at first – it will need inoculations to keep it healthy and a neutering operation at four to six months so as not to add to the number of unwanted kittens

Do you still want a kitten?

Or a cat? I've tried deliberately to put you off rushing into buying a kitten or cat. Why? Because you can go out and buy a new toy and play with it for a few days, then toss it aside. If you get bored with a toy, or break it, it doesn't really matter. A toy hasn't got feelings and doesn't care if it is ignored.

Living creatures do care. A kitten won't understand if you decide you don't really like it after all, or haven't time to play with it, or can't be bothered to understand it, or can't afford to keep it.

So only buy a kitten if you want a cat. Because your kitten will be a kitten for nine months and a cat for many, many years. During those years, it will be your friend if you are its friend. It will listen to all your secrets and tell no-one. It won't care what you look like or how badly you do at school. It will settle on your lap when you are feeling fed up and its silky fur and friendly purr will cheer you up again. It will sit on your books while you are doing your homework and rub its chin against you to show it cares. It will come rushing to greet you when it hears your footsteps. It will be *your* cat.

Are you ready to be its person?

Where will I buy my kitten?

From a friend? This is a good place to get a kitten and it's where most people get their kitten. Every year, especially during the summer months, thousands of cats have kittens and their owners go around asking all their friends if they would like a kitten. If you say yes, they'll be very relieved!

From a rescue shelter? This is usually the very best place to get a kitten. Maybe a quarter of a million cats and kittens find their way into rescue shelters each year – and only find their way out again if someone gives them a home. Kittens from a shelter are just as beautiful as any others and usually very healthy, because they have been well looked after by the shelter workers who know a lot about cats. If you visit a shelter but don't find the type of kitten you are looking for, they will let you know when the kitten you want *does* come in.

From a pet shop? Few pet shops sell kittens nowadays – for a very good reason. Cats and kittens are easily stressed – and the stress of being in a strange place with people staring at them can make them ill. If one of the kittens is unwell, the illness can spread quickly through all the kittens. The kittens may not always have been cared for expertly. And you cannot see the kittens' mother or find out anything about her. It really isn't a good idea to buy kittens from a pet shop – try a rescue shelter instead.

From a breeder? If you are buying a pedigree kitten, you should buy it from the person who bred it. The breeder will be able to tell you all about the kitten; what its personality is like, what its bad habits are, what its mum and dad are like,

and so on. Find a breeder you trust and then take their advice on the right kitten for you. Not every pedigree cat breeder is trustworthy however, so, before buying a kitten, contact the GCCF or CA (see page 96) to make sure you are buying from a reputable breeder. The GCCF and the CA will also be able to give you the names of cat clubs, where people who own the same breed of cat can learn more about them.

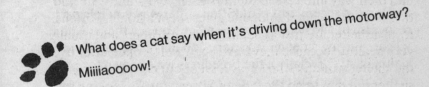

What does a cat say when it's driving down the motorway?

Miiiiaooooow!

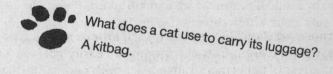

What does a cat use to carry its luggage?

A kitbag.

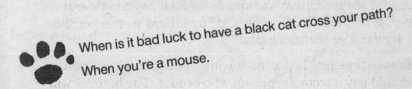

When is it bad luck to have a black cat cross your path?

When you're a mouse.

9

How do I choose a kitten?

How would you choose a bicycle or a skateboard? You'd spend a lot of time choosing the right one for you. You'd go to several shops to compare models and prices. You'd find one that was the right size for you, a colour you liked, with all the features you wanted.

So it seems sensible to spend at least as long choosing a kitten as choosing a bicycle. Don't decide you'd like a kitten and rush out to choose one the same day. Take your time and look at several litters of kittens; that way you'll learn to recognise fit and healthy kittens when you see them. And if you are buying a pedigree kitten, you may have to join a waiting list, especially if the breeder is well known for producing good kittens.

It's important to choose a healthy kitten because there are many feline illnesses which can kill. And, if you already have a cat, a sick kitten can pass on its illness and make your cat sick too. So, when you are buying a kitten, don't be afraid to check it over thoroughly. It should:

- be at least eight weeks old. A pedigree kitten will usually be twelve weeks old before it is sold and will always be inoculated, if you have bought it from a reputable breeder
- look healthy and happy. It should be curious and playful. It should have spent the first few months of its life living with its breeder's family, not shut in a pen, so it should not be nervous of people
- feel solid and strong. It should not be bony or have a pot-belly
- have clean, bright eyes with no sign of tears. Its nose should be clean, not running and it should not be

sneezing. If a kitten has runny eyes or sneezes, don't buy it (or any kitten from that household) as it may have a serious, or even fatal, illness

- have firm, white teeth and pink gums. Red gums may be inflamed and pale gums may be a sign the kitten is unwell
- have clean ears. Look inside the kitten's ears and sniff. There should be no smell and no brown wax. If the kitten is shaking its head or scratching its ears it may have an ear infection
- have clean fur which is not matted. Part its fur and look at its skin. If there are black specks on the skin, the kitten may have fleas
- have a clean bottom. Lift the kitten's tail and look. If the fur around its bottom is matted or yellowish, the kitten may have diarrhoea. This could be the symptom of a serious illness, although it may just be that the kitten has been overeating

The most important rule in buying a kitten is:
if in doubt, *do not buy*.

If the kitten is unwell with some minor problem, such as a tummy upset, you can always go back in a few days' time to look at it again, by which time it should be better. If it isn't, buy your kitten somewhere else.

You can ask the owner if they will allow you to take the kitten to a vet for a checkup *before* you decide whether or not to buy it (in which case you will have to pay the vet's fee whether you buy the kitten or not). If an owner won't allow you to do so, don't buy.

Remember that disease is easily spread from kitten to kitten by touch. If you are seeing several litters of kittens in one day, wash your hands thoroughly between visits and, if possible, change your clothes. Do this also when you get

back home if you already have a cat. Some pedigree cat breeders will ask you to leave your shoes at the door and to wash your hands before touching their kittens. Don't be offended – they are caring for their kittens' health.

Choose the right bicycle and you can have fun for a year or two before you outgrow it or it becomes unfashionable. Choose the right kitten and you've got a friend until you are an adult!

What type of cat?

Did you know that different types of cat have different personalities? Just as you would expect the behaviour of an Alsatian to be different from that of a poodle, so too the behaviour of a Siamese is different from that of a Persian. The care they need is different too. Although each cat is an individual, it is possible to divide cats into four broad types.

The Moggy
Non-pedigree cats are the most popular cats in the United Kingdom. They're easy to care for and need little grooming or special attention. They tend to be fairly independent and not so keen on sitting on laps as their pedigree cousins. However, they are really a lucky dip as far as temperament is concerned; some are very independent while others are real softies. If buying a moggy, try to meet its mother and, if possible, its father. This may give you some indication as to how the kitten will grow up.

British Shorthairs
If you don't know much about pedigree cats, you might think the British Shorthair is a moggy, because they do look quite like non-pedigree shorthairs. You can tell the difference because the British Shorthair should have a much rounder face and a lovely thick plush coat. It should also be quite large in size. British Shorthairs are easy to care for, friendly and much quieter than some other pedigrees, such as the Foreigns.

Foreign Shorthairs

The Siamese is the best-known of the Foreign Shorthairs but did you know there are versions of the Siamese which are all one colour, such as Havanas and Foreigns? Devon and Cornish Rex are also considered to be in this group, although they first appeared in the United Kingdom. The outstanding feature of the Foreign Shorthairs is their agility and activity. They are great climbers and acrobats and may climb curtains and even walls. They are demanding cats which love their owners and may expect an enormous amount of time and attention. They are also extremely clever, and their cunning often extends to opening the doors of food cupboards and refrigerators and helping themselves to the contents. They can be noisy, especially the Siamese.

Longhairs

These include Persians, Birmans, Ragdolls and other fluffy breeds. Longhairs are the lapcats – they love to settle down on an owner's lap and will stay there all day if allowed. They tend to be gentle, quiet and friendly, although kittens will be just as active and playful as any other breed. Some of the Longhairs tend not to be as clever as the Foreigns – which is not to say they are stupid, but they are definitely not as crafty. Their big disadvantage is that some of them, for example, the Persians, require a thorough combing every day or their coat will tangle and end up in knots. Others, such as the Ragdoll, have silky coats which require little grooming.

Some breeds of cat don't fall entirely within one group. For example, although the Balinese is a longhaired breed, it has Siamese ancestry, so it shares more traits with the Foreign Shorthairs than with the Longhairs. And longhaired cats, such as the Maine Coon, originally had moggy ancestry and still behave more like moggies than Longhairs. So when choosing a cat, think not just of its looks and its care needs but its ancestry. If in doubt, ask the breeder about the cat's background and always ask about any individual cat's temperament – they do vary.

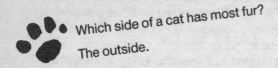

Which side of a cat has most fur?

The outside.

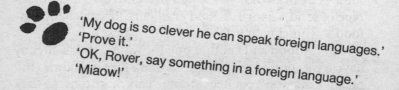

'My dog is so clever he can speak foreign languages.'
'Prove it.'
'OK, Rover, say something in a foreign language.'
'Miaow!'

What will my new kitten need?

Your kitten will be going to a new and very strange environment – your home. Until now, it has had the company of its brothers and sisters and the comfort of its mother. Now it will be going to a strange place, with strange people, strange smells and strange ways of doing things. So your new kitten will need:

- your company. You will have to take the place of its litter-mates until it is used to being part of *your* household. So it will enjoy playing with you – although it may want to play when you want to eat or do your homework. Then when you want to play, it will want to sleep because kittens need to sleep for eighteen to twenty hours a day. And it will need:
- some peace and quiet to get used to its new home. You will be dying to show your kitten to your friends – but try not to for a week or so. Let your kitten settle down in your home with your family before introducing it to new people. For this reason it isn't a good idea to buy a kitten at Christmas time or on a birthday if a party is planned.

Your kitten will also need:
- the same food as it is used to eating, at first. Ask the kitten's breeder what it has been given and give that food for a week or two. If you would prefer to give it another type of food, change its food gradually. If you change its food too quickly, it will have a tummy upset.
- a bowl for food and another one for water. If you already have a cat, don't expect them to share feeding bowls (or beds). Cats won't eat near strange cats or kittens, so they

will have to have separate bowls, placed several metres apart at first.

- A cosy bed. This needn't be expensive. It can be a clean cardboard box (one which has held tins or packets, not something smelly such as washing powder) with newspaper on the bottom for warmth, and an old blanket or sheet on top for comfort. The box and newspaper can be replaced regularly for hygiene and the blanket can be washed or replaced.

- a litter tray and litter. Kittens shouldn't go out of doors until at least a week after they've had their second inoculation (see page 18), so you will have to provide an indoor toilet for them. Even when they are old enough to go out of doors, cats should have a litter tray provided for night-time use, so that they can stay safely indoors at night.
- a scratching post. All cats need to scratch – it exercises their muscles and keeps their claws in good shape. If they are not given a scratching post and encouraged to use it,

they may scratch the furniture, which is a great deal more
expensive than a scratching post.

- a cat carrier. A carrier will be used every time you take
  your cat to the vet, to a holiday cattery or to a cat show.
  You will also need a carrier when you take your kitten
  home for the first time. A good carrier will last a lifetime,
  and your cat will be much happier using it than a
  cardboard box, which isn't really safe as a cat may claw its
  way out of it, or even fall out of it if it comes apart or
  becomes wet.

Of all these requirements, the first two are the most
important. Cats and kittens are very adaptable but they only
really thrive with love, understanding and companionship –
yours!

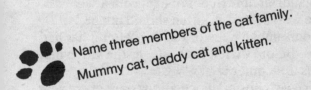

Name three members of the cat family.

Mummy cat, daddy cat and kitten.

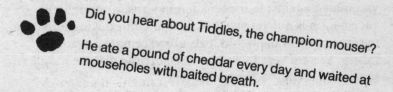

Did you hear about Tiddles, the champion mouser?

He ate a pound of cheddar every day and waited at
mouseholes with baited breath.

How do I keep my kitten healthy and safe?

When you were very young, you may have had a 'jab' – an inoculation or injection – to stop you catching certain diseases. Young kittens should have inoculations too, to stop them catching infectious enteritis and cat 'flu. Although the names of these illnesses don't sound too serious, either of them can kill a kitten or cat.

If you buy a pedigree kitten, it should be twelve weeks old and should already have had its inoculations. You should be given an inoculation certificate, signed by a vet, when you buy it. (If you don't, don't buy it.) If you buy a non-pedigree kitten, it will probably be younger (about eight weeks), and won't have had its inoculations. It should be taken to the vet for its first inoculation at nine weeks of age, with a second inoculation three weeks later. A kitten should not be allowed out of doors until a week or ten days after it has had *both* inoculations. Before that, it isn't safe, as the kitten may pick up infections from other cats.

Cats should receive 'booster' inoculations once every year to keep them free from these serious illnesses. (In other countries, cats and kittens receive other inoculations as well as those for infectious enteritis and cat 'flu. They can be vaccinated against feline leukaemia virus, although this vaccination is not yet available in the United Kingdom. And in some parts of the world, cats are vaccinated against rabies. We are very lucky that this terrible disease hasn't reached the United Kingdom – yet.)

When you take your kitten to be inoculated, your vet will give it a check-up. If you have bought a kitten which is

already inoculated, make an appointment to see the vet anyway, just for a health check. Your vet will recommend worming, if necessary (see page 21). If your kitten has any ailments, such as an ear infection or teething problems, your vet will be able to treat them and advise you on any special care needs.

He or she will also advise you of the best time to have your kitten neutered; usually around four to six months for a female kitten and four to nine months for a male kitten (see page 29).

Your kitten will stay healthy and well on good quality tinned or fresh food and may need the addition of a vitamin and mineral supplement (see page 23 for diet). A bowl of clean water should always be available. Don't give your kitten milk; after four weeks of age it doesn't need milk and it may give it an upset tummy.

Keep your kitten safe by checking your house for danger. Remember that kittens are very curious and get into all sorts of trouble just by being nosey. They will climb up chimneys and squeeze through gaps in open windows or doors. If the door of the washing-machine is left open, they will climb in

there and may fall asleep on the washing. Kittens have been drowned when the washing machine has been switched on. So always check that your kitten isn't inside any electrical appliance before you switch on. Keep the lid down on the loo too; kittens can fall in and be unable to get out again.

Don't leave plastic bags lying around or opened tins of cat food – even if they're empty. Kittens can suffocate inside a plastic bag or cut their faces on the sharp edge of a tin when they stick their heads inside to lick out the remains of the food. If you're sewing, never leave the needle threaded because a kitten will play with the thread. Once it gets into its mouth, the kitten isn't able to spit it out again and the thread will be swallowed – complete with needle.

Kittens are just like very young toddlers; they really have no sense at all. For the first few months of their lives they will depend on *you* to keep them safe. So try to look around your home with a kitten's eyes and remove anything with which they might get into mischief.

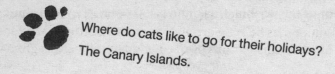

Where do cats like to go for their holidays?
The Canary Islands.

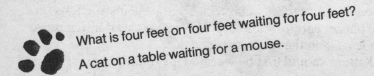

What is four feet on four feet waiting for four feet?
A cat on a table waiting for a mouse.

What if my kitten has worms?

Worms are nothing to worry about as long as they are treated as soon as you suspect your kitten (or cat) has them. Every cat will have roundworms at some time in its life and kittens will be born with roundworms.

Worms live in a cat's intestines where they can prevent it getting full nourishment from its food. Kittens can swallow worm eggs while suckling from their mothers, or cats can swallow prey with worm larvae inside them. Worms can kill kittens if not treated because they can form such a solid mass that the intestines become blocked.

Symptoms may include:
- pot-bellies (especially in kittens)
- poor condition – fur which looks rough and doesn't shine
- diarrhoea or vomiting
- lack of interest in food and weight loss
- constipation
- coughing
- tapeworms, which are not as common as roundworms, can sometimes be seen around your cat's bottom – they look like brownish grains of rice and may still be wriggling

Treatment
Worms can be treated by tablets or pills which can be bought at pet stores or from your vet. Roundworms and tapeworms need different types of tablets. Follow the instructions on the packet carefully and don't give your cat or kitten more (or less) than the recommended dose.

Kittens should first be wormed for roundworms at around four to six weeks of age and wormed again every month until they are six months old. From six to twelve months, they can

be wormed every other month, then two or three times a year after that. Only worm for tapeworms if you suspect your cat or kitten *has* tapeworms. If it has, burn its bedding, because bits of the tapeworm may have dropped off there.

You can break worming pills in half to make them easier to swallow. Many worming treatments are 'palatable' – they taste nice to a cat – so they can be broken up and mixed with food, or simply placed in the cat's bowl for it to eat. If using palatable worming treatments, watch while your cat eats to make sure it eats all of it.

And, of course, after worming your cat (or even just playing with it) don't forget to wash your hands.

> There was a wee bit mousikie
> What dwelt in Gilberatie-O
> That couldna get a bite o cheese
> For Cheetie-Pussie-Cattie-O
>
> Quo' mousie tae the cheesikie,
> 'O fain wad I be at ye, O,
> If 'twerena for the shairpent claws
> O' Cheetie-Pussie-Cattie-O'
> *Scottish nursery rhyme*

What do I feed my kitten?

Kittens need good-quality food which is high in protein – proteins are the 'building blocks' of the body. Nowadays several companies make tinned food specially for kittens, although you won't usually find this in supermarkets. Your local pet store will have it in stock or will order it for you.

Good-quality tinned cat food will be all right too, but you should add a vitamin and mineral supplement to the food in the correct quantities recommended on the container according to your kitten's age. (Neutered *adult* cats which are fed on a good diet don't need a supplement.) To choose a good cat food, read the labels carefully and pick one which is high in protein, low in ash (mineral) content and preferably doesn't contain any cereal or soy products. Cereal and soy add protein to the diet but it is a lower-quality protein than the protein in meat or fish. Don't just choose the most expensive tin – you may be paying for advertising, not what is inside. Any ready-prepared cat food you buy should be labelled a 'complete' food. If it is a 'supplementary' food it won't contain everything your kitten or cat needs for good health, so should only be fed occasionally.

Fresh food can be fed too, although tinned food is just as good (and in some cases better) for your kitten. For example, if you fed your kitten nothing but cod, it would not receive enough vitamin D or E and would become ill. You can occasionally give your kitten a little fish, or a small amount of liver or kidney, or a little raw mince (mince for humans – not pet mince which must never be served raw), a little cheese or cooked egg. This need not be expensive. For example, if you are having roast chicken to eat, you may not

like the skin or some of the darker meat. Your kitten will! (Just make sure *all* bones are removed or your kitten could choke.) If you are having a chop or cutlet, you may not like the fatty bit. Your kitten will love it and fat does a feline no harm at all. If you are having fish, your kitten will enjoy eating the cooked skin and the little fiddly bits you can't be bothered with. Again, do remove the bones. And always feed your kitten in its bowl, at its proper mealtimes – never give scraps from the table.

There are other types of food for cats and kittens too. There are 'gourmet' or luxury foods which come in very small tins. These are a real treat for a kitten and are usually very high in protein, so they are good for them. However, no kitten needs to be fed gourmet food *all* the time – although your kitten may try to convince you that it does! Again, shop around for the best bargains in gourmet foods. Compare prices and tin sizes – you can make quite a saving by careful shopping.

Dry foods are becoming popular now because they are so easy to feed. They are clean to dish up and don't go off in hot weather. Cats *must* drink extra water when they are given dry foods. Some of the dry foods encourage felines to drink more but some don't. Steer clear of the ones which don't. I prefer to feed cats tinned food with just half a dozen pieces of dry food sprinkled on top to exercise their teeth.

There are also 'semi-moist' cat foods, which come in packets, but they have never become very popular in the United Kingdom, most owners preferring to use tinned food. There are also 'chubs' which are large, sausage-like plastic containers. Chubs are usually not complete cat foods, so should not be fed too often.

How much should you feed your kitten? A small kitten can't eat very much at one time so should be fed four times a

day until it is about eight to ten weeks old. It can have three
meals a day until it is four or five months old and after that
feed it twice a day. Don't feed too much at one meal; start
with a tablespoon of food and gradually increase amounts as
your kitten grows. If its tummy is bulging out on all sides
after a meal, you're feeding it too much. Another sign that a
kitten may be being overfed is if it starts to defecate – make
a mess – outside its litter tray.

Give your kitten its last meal of the day just before
bedtime. If it goes out of doors during the day, this will
ensure it comes in for the night. (Cats shouldn't spend the
night out of doors. They are likely to become lost, stolen or
run over. At best, they will have a cold, miserable time.)
Give your kitten a good variety of food so that it doesn't
become a fussy eater.

Beware of feeding your cat dog food. It is cheaper – but it
isn't nourishing enough for a cat. Dog food doesn't have
enough of a substance called *taurine* in it – dogs can make
taurine in their bodies but cats can't. Without taurine in its
diet, a cat will go blind. A cat will also go blind if fed on a
completely vegetarian diet because it will not have sufficient
taurine. Don't feed your cat liver more than once a week.
Some cats become addicted to liver and refuse to eat
anything else. They end up very ill from an overdose of
vitamin A.

Let your kitten or cat have a quiet place to eat and its own
bowl, which should be wider than its whiskers. If the bowl is
too narrow, your cat may trail the food onto the floor to eat
it. Bowls should be washed regularly in diluted household
bleach, then thoroughly rinsed to remove all smell.

What about drinks? Kittens and cats are still given milk to
drink but this is a very old-fashioned idea. Once a kitten has
been weaned from its mother, it doesn't need milk, as long

as it is being fed a good diet. In fact, milk gives many cats diarrhoea because they are allergic to the lactose in the milk. Water is all they need to drink.

A clean bowl of water should be available at all times and refilled regularly, even if you never see your cat drinking from it. If your cat is thirsty, it will drink. Cats aren't silly!

'What's your cat's name?'
'Ben Hur.'
'That's a funny name for a cat.'
'Well, we called him just Ben until he had kittens . . .'

What do you call an overweight, striped cat?

A flabby tabby.

How do I housetrain my kitten?

It usually isn't necessary to do any housetraining as kittens and cats are extremely clean – unless there is a problem (see page 62). As soon as kittens are able to walk they will find their way to their litter tray and use it. One thing which is necessary, however, is to *provide* a litter tray. This is essential until your kitten is old enough to go out of doors (a week after its second inoculation, see page 18) and it makes life easier for your kitten if you continue to provide a tray after that time.

Kittens can't wait if they need to go to the toilet. If it is a long way to the cat flap or they have to wait around until someone opens the door for them, a corner of the carpet will probably be used instead. If this happens, don't scold or punish your kitten – it really couldn't help soiling the floor. If you are cross it will only make your kitten nervous. Instead, you should clean any mess on the floor and wash it thoroughly to remove the smell. If the smell remains, the kitten will remember that that corner is its toilet and will use it again.

Place the litter tray in a convenient place. If your kitten is very young or your home is large, you may have to provide several trays, or move a tray from room to room as the kitten moves around. A litter tray isn't particularly pretty to look at so you can place it inside an upended box with a small doorway cut in it or buy one of the newer, covered litter trays. If your kitten scatters litter on the floor, place the tray inside a shallow box and that will help keep the floor clean.

Litter trays cost less than a pound and can be bought at pet stores and in supermarkets. Or you could use a clean

seed tray or even an old washing-up bowl if it is large enough (don't use it afterwards for washing the dishes!). Litter can be bought in the same places and is often cheaper from pet stores if you buy it in large quantities. The most common type of litter looks like small grey or white lumps. This is a natural clay, taken out of the ground and dried. This type of litter works best if it is used to a depth of about 8 cm because any liquid will form a ball and is easily lifted out. Another type of litter is made from sawdust, pressed into pellets. When it becomes wet, it dissolves into sawdust again. This type of litter should be used in a shallow layer as it expands when it is wet. If you run out of litter you can use torn-up newspaper or shredded paper kitchen towels, or even clean soil from the garden, or peat.

Trays can be cleaned out by using a scoop which can be bought where you bought your tray. Or you can use an old slotted kitchen spoon. Both types of litter can be flushed down the toilet in small amounts, wrapped and placed in a bin, or put on the compost heap. The wooden type can also be burned.

It's possible to buy deodoriser to sprinkle on litter but many cats don't like this and may use the floor instead of the litter. There are many other reasons why cats or kittens may soil the floor – see page 62 – and probably the most common reason is that the tray isn't clean. If possible, trays should be cleaned out each time they're used (after all, we don't like using dirty toilets so why should a cat). If that isn't possible, they should be cleaned out twice a day.

Housetraining a kitten is much simpler than housetraining a puppy and, with luck, you should have no problems (or puddles) at all.

Should I let my cat have kittens?

This is a question you should think about while your kitten is still very young. Some cats are really still kittens when they are able to have kittens themselves, so if you wait more than six months you may have no choice in the matter. (With a female Siamese, or part-Siamese, if you wait more than four months it may be too late – Siamese grow up *very* quickly.)

Some people think that a female cat, or queen, should have at least one litter of kittens because it is 'good for her'. This isn't true. Having kittens is painful and takes up a lot of your cat's energy and strength. Some people believe that neutered cats 'become fat'. This isn't true either. Cats only become fat if they are fed too much. And some people think it is 'cruel' to have a cat neutered. Nothing could be further from the truth. The operation doesn't hurt and cats don't feel they are missing anything afterwards. Cruelty is allowing a cat to have kittens – just visit any cat rescue shelter and see the thousands of cats and kittens which don't have homes or anyone to love them to see what I mean. Even if you find homes for the kittens your cat has had, those kittens will be depriving other kittens of homes, because there are just too many kittens around.

Many people let their cat have kittens intending to keep one of the kittens for company for their cat. This isn't a good idea either as mums and grown-up kittens usually can't stand the sight of each other! It's a much better idea to visit a cat rescue shelter and give some other cat a home.

Don't let the expense of neutering put you off – neutering a cat can save you a lot of money. Male cats, for example, get into fights over female cats and are sometimes injured and need veterinary treatment. Or, chasing females, they

can run in front of a car and be seriously hurt, requiring hundreds of pounds' worth of veterinary treatment. Neutered males also live longer than those which aren't and they're much nicer to have around. Unneutered tomcats spray strong-smelling urine everywhere – including all around their home – to mark their territory.

The operation for neutering a female cat (called spaying) is slightly more complicated and consequently a little more expensive. However, if you allow your cat to become pregnant, you could end up with massive bills if anything goes wrong during the pregnancy or birth, or if the kittens fall ill.

If you really can't afford the cost of neutering or spaying, contact your local animal or cat charity. They will often help with the cost if they can. They would rather pay for a cat to be neutered than be asked to find homes for the resulting kittens.

Ask your vet about spaying or neutering when your kitten goes for its inoculations or its first check-up. Males are neutered at any time between four to nine months. Female kittens are usually spayed between four to six months, although sometimes the operation is carried out at three months.

Don't leave the spaying of a female kitten any longer than six months. If you do, one day you might discover that your kitten is rolling around on the ground, making frightening howling noises, or lying at a strange angle with her bottom sticking in the air. Many owners, seeing this for the first time, think that their cat has been run over, has broken her back, or is in terrible pain. None of these is true. In fact, the cat is 'calling'. This means she is sexually mature and is ready and keen to mate with a male cat.

If you don't want her to have kittens, you must keep her

indoors until she stops calling, and keep her away from all unneutered male cats. This is easier said than done as calling cats have only one thing on their minds – they want to mate. They become very crafty and can sneak out of a barely-open door as quick as a flash. The first 'call' will last around five to seven days and, while it is going on, make an appointment for spaying with your vet for *after* the calling finishes. Cats cannot be spayed while they are still calling as it is more likely that there would be complications then. Get your cat to the vet as soon as you can when her call is over and don't allow her to call another time. Constant calling, without being mated, can damage your cat's health.

If you were too late this time, turn to page 74 for advice on kittening!

> Poussie, poussie, baudrons,
> Where hae ye been?
> I've been to London
> To see the Queen!
>
> Poussie, poussie, baudrons,
> What got ye there?
> I got a guid fat mousikie
> Runnin' up a stair!
>
> Poussie, poussie, baudrons,
> What did ye do wi't?
> I put it in my meal-pock,
> To eat it to my bread!
> *Scottish nursery rhyme*

Records

The **biggest** domestic breed of cat is the Ragdoll. Males can weigh more than 9 kg (20 lbs) when fully grown and females can weigh up to 6.8 kg (15 lbs). This is approximately three times the weight of an average-size cat.

The **smallest** domestic breed of cat is probably the Singapura, from Singapore, where it has been called 'the drain cat' because it lived in small drainage pipes. An adult female might weigh as little as 1.8 kg (4 lbs).

The **fattest** cat was Himmy, an Australian cat who weighed more than 20 kg (45 lb). He had a waist measurement of 81.2 cm (32 in) which is several inches bigger than the waist of an average human female. His owner said Himmy wasn't a greedy cat and didn't eat much!

The **oldest** cat was probably a Devon tabby called Ma. She lived to be 34 years 5 months old. The owner of an American cat claimed it was 37 years old but, on investigation, the 37-year-old cat turned out to be three different cats whose ages had been added together!

The **largest litter of kittens** was one of nineteen born to a Burmese mother and a half-Siamese father. Fifteen kittens survived. Cats only have eight teats to feed their kittens and it has been known for cats with large litters to divide the kittens into two groups and arrange two 'sittings' for meals.

The average size of a litter of kittens is around four or five, although a cat's first litter is usually smaller. Two, three, four, or even five litters can be produced by one cat in a year. One cat gave birth to 420 kittens in the course of her lifetime. Allowing a cat to have lots of kittens is unfair to her and to the kittens as it is difficult to find homes for them and they often end up unwanted and homeless.

The **most mice caught by a cat** totalled more than 23,000 for a cat called Towser who worked at a distillery in Scotland until the mid-1980s. Fifty years previously, the **rat catching record** was won by Minnie, who killed 12,480 rats at the White City Stadium in London.

The **fastest** a cat has been known to run is 27 miles an hour over a distance of 59 metres. This is 2 miles an hour faster than a human sprinter. Cat racing took place in England in the 1930s and 1940s on special tracks with the cats chasing an electric mouse. However, when a newspaper printed an April Fool joke in the 1980s pretending that a new cat racing track was to be built, it was deluged with complaints from people who thought the idea was cruel.

The **cat who travelled furthest** was Princess Truman Tao-Tai, a sailing Siamese who lived on board a British iron-ore carrier. She travelled one and a half million sea miles, 2,400,000 km, during her sixteen-year lifetime, during which she never left the ship because of quarantine regulations.

The **most expensive** cat in the world is the Sphynx, which is also the rarest. The Sphynx isn't covered with fur but with a fine down and there are only about twenty Sphynx in the world. It is very rare for a Sphynx cat to be sold but if one was, it would probably cost about £4000. The next most expensive cat is the California Spangled Cat, a spotted cat bred in America which costs about £1000.

Do I have to comb or brush my cat?

It is a very good idea to comb or brush most cats once a week or so, and it is absolutely essential with some breeds. The Persian, for example, with its long, thick fur, must be combed thoroughly every day, or its fur will tangle and end up in knots. Even cats with short fur benefit from a regular combing, especially in spring and early summer when they moult.

Cats groom themselves with their tongues and most manage to keep themselves looking smart. However, a cat's tongue is covered in tiny barbs on which loose fur catches, just like a comb. The cat swallows this hair and can end up with a hairball (also called a furball) in its stomach. You may have seen a cat trying to get rid of a hairball; it may eat some grass or a plant to make itself sick then vomit it up. Although this isn't a pleasant sight it is necessary if the cat has swallowed a lot of loose hair. Otherwise the hairball would cause a blockage in the intestines and the cat would be unable to eat. This happens if the cat is unable to get rid of the hairball and sometimes an operation is needed to remove it. If your cat has the beginnings of a hairball, you can buy a hairball treatment from your pet store. Follow directions carefully and see your vet if the hairball isn't expelled within twenty-four hours.

So regular combing or brushing prevents your cat swallowing loose hair which builds up into hairballs. Start combing your kitten when it is young, so that it becomes used to it. To start with, just run your hands over its fur as if you were stroking it. This is much the same motion as grooming with a comb. When it is used to you running your hands over its fur, run a comb over its fur. A metal-toothed

pet comb is the best thing to use.

Start and finish with your kitten's favourite spots, which may be under the chin, on the tummy or behind the ears. Your kitten will then remember that grooming is fun and won't object to it. If your kitten is in a playful mood, it may try to play with the comb. Don't let it do so, or it will always want to play and make grooming very difficult. Put the comb down for the time being and try again later when your kitten is feeling less playful.

If a longhaired kitten or cat isn't groomed regularly, its fur will tangle and end up knotted and matted. These knots are very difficult to remove. If the matt is small, combing may be enough to remove it. The knot should be combed out piece by piece starting on the outside and working inwards as the fur untangles. Care needs to be taken not to hurt the cat. A bigger knot may need to be cut off and you should ask an adult to do this for you. It should be done very carefully, so that the cat isn't cut if it should begin to struggle. Although there may be an unsightly patch where the fur was cut off, the fur will grow again. Sometimes longhaired cats are found with fur which is completely matted because the owners haven't groomed them for ages. These cats have to be anaesthetised by a vet, who shaves off all the fur while the cat is asleep. It would be too distressing for the cats to be shaved while awake.

Is any other grooming necessary? When you comb your kitten, check that its ears are clean. Most cats manage to keep their ears very clean but some of the pedigree breeds – especially those with big ears – get quite dirty and their ears need to be cleaned at least once a week. Cotton wool is the safest thing to use for ear-cleaning, dampened with a little oil, but it isn't always easy to get out all the wax with cotton wool. Cotton buds can be used but it is vital that they are held vertically (upright) and are not pushed down into the ear canal which would hurt your kitten. It's quite a tricky thing to do, especially if your kitten is wriggling, so it might be a good idea to get an adult to do it.

Another piece of grooming where adult assistance would be useful is claw trimming. This is when just the very tip of the claws are trimmed off to blunt them, either to stop you or your furniture being scratched. (However, cats always want to sharpen up their trimmed claws again and they do so by stropping – often on the furniture.) Hold your cat firmly, place your thumb on top of the paw and your finger on the pawpad underneath. Press gently and the claws will

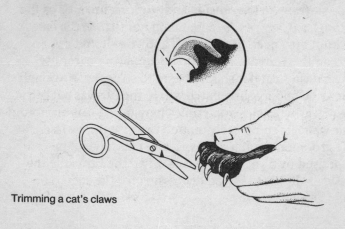

Trimming a cat's claws

unsheath. Take off just the very tip using nail scissors, nail clippers or claw trimmers. Be very careful not to take off more than the tip. There is a pinkish-coloured quick inside the claw which, if it is cut into, will bleed copiously.

Only the front claws are trimmed; the back claws are usually left to look after themselves.

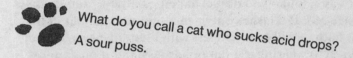

What do you call a cat who sucks acid drops?
A sour puss.

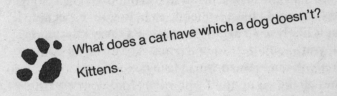

What does a cat have which a dog doesn't?

Kittens.

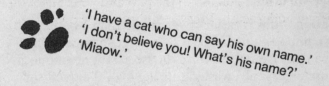

'I have a cat who can say his own name.'
'I don't believe you! What's his name?'
'Miaow.'

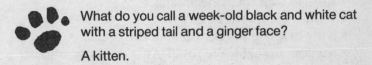

What do you call a week-old black and white cat with a striped tail and a ginger face?

A kitten.

Will I ever have to bath my cat?

Cats are usually very good at keeping themselves clean, but sometimes they do need help. If a cat gets particularly muddy, or oily, or its fur is soiled by diarrhoea, it shouldn't be left to lick it off.

If your cat is likely to object to being bathed, trim its claws (see page 36). If it lashes out in an attempt to get out of the sink or bath, it will hurt you less with blunted claws. If your cat is used to wearing a collar or harness, put it on your cat and use it to help keep hold of it (don't use a flea collar). You'll need an apron or a towel tied around you to keep you dry and you should have someone to help you, especially if your cat is likely to struggle. If your cat's fur is knotted or matted, you should get rid of the matts before you bath it or the water will make them worse (see page 34).

Gather all the equipment you will need before you begin. You will need:

- a sink – this is easier to reach into than a bath
- shampoo – this can be a special cat shampoo which you can buy from a pet store, or use a baby shampoo. Don't use detergents, washing-up liquid or dandruff shampoos
- several towels to dry your cat
- a piece of towelling or a rubber mat for the bottom of the sink, to stop your cat slipping
- bowls of hand-warm water
- a jug to scoop water over your cat
- a warm, draught-free room in which to dry your cat

First, place 5 cm–10 cm hand-warm water in the bottom of a sink in which you have placed the towelling or rubber mat. Test the temperature as you would for a baby's bath – dip

your elbow into the water. Pour a little shampoo into this water. This makes it easier to wet your cat's fur right down to the skin.

Lift your cat into the sink and hold it steady with one hand while you scoop water over it from the jug (this is much easier if someone is helping you). Start by pouring just a little water over your cat's legs, working up the body until all except the head is wet. If the head has to be washed, use a dampened sponge. All the time you are doing this, talk soothingly to your cat. If it is unused to being bathed it may be quite frightened until it realises no harm will come to it.

Once your cat is completely wet, lather in the shampoo, again avoiding the head. Then rinse thoroughly by pouring clean water from the bowls over your cat, using the jug to do so. If your cat is particularly dirty, you may have to repeat the shampooing and rinsing but usually one shampoo is enough. Let the water out of the sink before you rinse your cat off. Rinsing can be done more easily by using a shower attachment but, as these make a hissing noise, many cats won't tolerate them.

Wrap your cat in a towel and dry it as much as possible. Your cat may shake itself like a dog to get rid of the water, so make sure you are still in a room which is easily dried (such as a kitchen or bathroom). Then wrap your cat in another, dry towel and rub dry again. Some cats like to be wrapped in yet another, dry towel until their fur dries out because, until it does, a cat will feel very chilly. Make sure it is kept warm and stays indoors the rest of the day and night.

If your cat is just a little grubby you can give it a dry shampoo, which is particularly useful if its fur is sticky or greasy. You needn't buy a dry shampoo; you can use talcum powder or cat litter. The grey type of litter, called Fuller's Earth, has been used for thousands of years as a cosmetic

and dry shampoo. Simply grind some up into a powder. If using talcum powder, try to choose an unscented brand. Sprinkle it on to your cat's coat, taking care not to get it into your cat's eyes, nose or mouth, and rub it in. Then you can immediately brush it out again, and it will take out grease, dirt and dust with it. Make sure it is brushed out thoroughly.

If you're lucky you will never have to bath your cat. Many cats live clean lives without ever going near water.

Top cats

There are approximately six and a half million cats in the United Kingdom and very few of those are pedigree cats. (Pedigree cats are those belonging to a specific breed, whose ancestry is known and the names of whose parents, grandparents, great grandparents and great-great grandparents is written down on a piece of paper called a pedigree certificate.)

Non-pedigree cats are by far the most popular, as around 93 per cent of all cats in this country are non-pedigrees. When *Going Live!* viewers helped me with the cat fur colour survey in 1987, I discovered that 92 per cent of viewers had non-pedigree cats and the remaining 8 per cent had pedigree cats. Here is the top ten pedigree breeds owned by *Going Live!* viewers. Next to this is the top ten pedigree breeds as compiled by the United Kingdom Feline Register (UKFR).

Going Live! viewers' cats	UKFR statistics
1 Siamese	Persian
2 Burmese	Siamese
3 Persian	British Shorthair
4 British Shorthair	Birman
5 Colourpoint	Burmese
6 Birman	Abyssinian
7 Foreign	Colourpoint
8 Chinchilla	Foreign
9 British Blue	Chinchilla
10 Abyssinian	Rex

I wanted to find out the most common colours of non-pedigree cats and to see if there were more cats of one colour in one part of the country than another. This is what the *Going Live!* cat colour survey showed to be the top ten fur colours.

1 Black and white	6 Ginger and white
2 Black	7 Tortoiseshell and white
3 Tabby	8 Tabby and white
4 Ginger	9 White
5 Tortoiseshell	10 Blue (grey)

Black and white cats – and black cats – outnumber all other colours and make up two in five of the United Kingdom's cat population. The black and white cats stretch throughout the country from Land's End to John O'Groats, including Wales. Northern Ireland was one of the few places where there were more tabbies than any other colour.

However, there is a golden band stretching *across* the country from Essex, Herefordshire and Warwickshire to Wales, where there are many ginger or tortoiseshell cats.

What do I do if my cat has fleas?

All cats have fleas at some time or another and it is nothing to be embarrassed about as long as the fleas are treated as soon as they're seen. Fleas live part of the time on your cat and part of the time in carpets, furnishings and cracks in the floorboards – which is what makes them so difficult to get rid of.

The first sign that your cat has fleas may be little black, dusty specks in the fur. These are flea droppings. Because they contain your cat's blood, they will turn red if dropped on to a wet tissue. They may be found anywhere on the fur, but particularly around the neck, mouth, ears and tail of your cat. The fleas themselves aren't often seen but are tiny, reddish-brown insects. If you see your cat scratching (usually around the chin) you can almost guarantee it has fleas. Of course, if your cat is dark in colour, you won't see the dark-coloured flea faeces in its fur. So comb your cat when it is standing on a light-coloured surface; you will then see any dark specks which drop off.

You may discover your cat has fleas when *you* get bitten – most likely around the ankles and wrists. This is unpleasant and itchy for a day or two, but at least cat fleas don't live on humans (they will take a bite then jump off again) because they much prefer the taste of cats.

As soon as fleas are discovered, they must be treated. Cats with fleas will soon become weak and ill, and fleas can transmit serious diseases and help infest your cat with worms.

There are many different flea treatments available but the most commonly used are flea sprays and powders.

Because most cats don't like being treated with flea

42

preparations and may fight or scratch, ask an adult to do it for you. Don't use flea spray in the same room as a fish tank (it can kill the fish) and don't spray in the same room as food or water bowls. Don't allow the spray to go into your cat's eyes, ears or mouth and try not to breathe it in. Always wash hands thoroughly after using flea preparations.

If spraying a cat, hold it firmly but gently by the scruff of the neck while it has all four feet on the ground. Spray a two- to three-second burst along its back then along its tummy. It isn't necessary to cover every inch of fur as fleas will die when they come into contact with the treated areas.

If using a flea powder, sprinkle it on, keeping it away from the cat's face. Then brush it out thoroughly. If your cat really objects to being treated for fleas, it can be placed inside an old pillowcase containing some flea powder; its head must be outside the pillowcase.

Flea collars are popular with many owners, while others refuse to use them. Flea collars work by releasing insecticide over your cat's fur, so your cat is constantly in contact with the insecticide and it is possible for the skin around its neck to become irritated. Always remove a flea collar if it becomes wet and take it off for at least a few hours each day to allow the skin to 'breathe'. Remember too that cats can be trapped by their collars if the collar catches on a fence or branch.

There are also herbal products which are made specially to repel cat fleas. These don't kill the fleas, they simply keep them away from your cat, so it is important to make sure there are no fleas around in the environment (see below). Advertisements for these products can be found in cat magazines.

The old-fashioned way of removing fleas is to comb the cat with a fine-toothed flea comb, removing any fleas and

43

burning them. This is a long and laborious process but is totally safe for everyone concerned, except for the fleas.

That's how to treat your cat for fleas but, because fleas live part of their lives away from the cat, the cat's environment must also be treated. If it isn't, new fleas will hatch within a few days or weeks and your cat will be scratching again.

Special sprays are available to treat the environment and kill any fleas in furniture or carpets. This type of spray may be called a 'space and surface spray', a 'household' spray or a 'residual' spray. It can be sprayed on furnishings and will kill any fleas or flea eggs without damaging the furnishings. Again, don't inhale the spray, remove fish tanks and food and water bowls – and all people and pets. Leave the treated room closed for at least half an hour then air it thoroughly before allowing anyone inside. Wash or burn your cat's bedding as fleas may be lurking there.

Don't use this sort of spray on your cat – it is for furnishings only.

Many people spray their cats and their cat's environment weekly. I feel this is overkill. There's an American expression – 'if it ain't broke don't fix it'. The answer to killing fleas lies somewhere between waging weekly chemical warfare and waiting for your cat to scratch.

Legends

The legend of the Siamese

The Siamese is the most popular cat in the United Kingdom today but hundreds of years ago it was so rare and considered so beautiful that only Siamese (Siam is now Thailand) royalty were allowed to keep a Siamese. The cats lived in palaces and were rarely seen by the common people.

Some Siamese cats have a kink – a bend – in their tail. According to legend, a princess was bathing in a stream with her pet Siamese waiting on the river bank. The princess thought her rings might slip off in the water but she had nowhere to put them for safekeeping. Her Siamese obligingly crooked his tail so that she could place them on it – and the Siamese has had a kinked tail ever since.

The cross-eyes of some Siamese are said to come from the time they were used in palaces as guard-cats. They were set to guard a valuable vase which they watched with such concentration that their eyes crossed and remained that way evermore. The truth is that a defect in blue eyes causes some blue-eyed cats to see double. Only by deliberately crossing their eyes can they see clearly.

The legend of the cat's purr

A prince was captured by an evil baron and threatened with death. The baron said he would let the prince go only if he could find someone to spin 10 000 hanks of thread within a month.

His girlfriend (who was, of course, a princess and, fortunately, a princess who knew how to spin) said that she would spin the thread and save him. She soon realised the task was hopeless – one person alone could not spin so much thread. So she asked her cats to help.

They all worked without ceasing and finished spinning the thread just in time to save the prince.

The princess got her prince back safely and her cats were rewarded by the gift of the purr – the same noise made by a whirring spinning wheel.

If six copycats were sitting on a wall and one jumped off, how many would be left?

None – being copycats they'd *all* jump off.

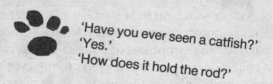

'Have you ever seen a catfish?'
'Yes.'
'How does it hold the rod?'

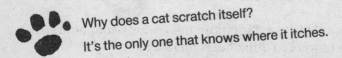

Why does a cat scratch itself?

It's the only one that knows where it itches.

How do I know if my cat is ill?

It isn't always as easy as you might think to know if a cat is ill. They're such 'macho' creatures that they can be very ill indeed before it is obvious that anything at all is bothering them. The better you know your cat or kitten, the quicker you will realise that something is wrong.

A change of behaviour is often the first sign of illness. If your cat is usually a friendly purrbag but suddenly becomes unfriendly, or if a hearty eater ignores its food, or your cat, instead of playing, droops in a corner looking sorry for itself, keep a close watch on it. If it doesn't look better next day, or if other symptoms appear, visit your vet as soon as possible.

What are the symptoms of illness? If your cat . . .

- is coughing or sneezing, and has runny eyes or nose
- or its third eyelid (at the inside corner of its eye) is showing, or there is a film over its eye
- or it is vomiting or has diarrhoea for more than twenty-four hours
- or it is unable to eat for more than twenty-four hours, or seems to want to drink but is unable to
- or it is frothing at the mouth or drooling (don't confuse

this with dribbling, which many cats do when happy)
- or it is very thirsty and drinking a lot
- or it is urinating very frequently
- or its urine or faeces has blood in it
- or it is straining in its litter tray but is unable to pass anything
- or it has any swellings, lumps or deep wounds
- or it is staggering, paralysed, or having a fit
- or its breathing becomes difficult
- or it constantly scratches its ears
- or it appears to be in pain
- or if you're just worried about its health . . .

contact your vet immediately

A vet will never mind examining an animal which turns out to be perfectly healthy – he or she would much prefer that should happen than a sick animal not receive necessary treatment. (I was very worried once when one of my cats developed a large lump on her side. I took her to the vet straight away but, when I got to the surgery, the vet couldn't find any sign of a lump. Then I realised that the lump must have been my cat's lunch, working its way through her intestines!)

If you are worried about the cost of veterinary treatment, there are many branches of the People's Dispensary for Sick Animals (PDSA) throughout the country. They will provide free veterinary treatment for animals belonging to people receiving benefits.

If you don't qualify for free treatment, you can buy pet health insurance for your cat. For a yearly or quarterly premium, all veterinary bills for illness and accident will be paid by the insurance company. (They won't pay for the cost of inoculations, neutering, or in most cases the costs of

48

kittening.) There are a number of insurance companies which provide policies for pets and they provide different cover for different prices, so shop around for the best one for you. Vets usually have leaflets in their surgery which will give you information about insurance.

Strange but true

Dick Whittington's cat probably had sails rather than four legs. Dick became Lord Mayor of London in the 15th century, but he was also a coal merchant. In those days, coal was transported on large barges, called cats. So Dick Whittington's cat may have been very important to him . . . but not for the reasons we thought!

The first cat show was held at the Crystal Palace in 1871. In the early days, owners often paraded their cats on ribbon leashes around a ring – a very unhygienic practice which led to many feline illnesses and even deaths. Owners didn't have to attend the early shows personally and sometimes would send their cats to a show by train, nailed up in wooden boxes.

The British Royal Family have always been more fond of dogs than cats although Queen Victoria owned several Persians. She had two Blue Persians and a White Persian called White Heather. Our present Queen Elizabeth was given a Siamese kitten called Holly as a Christmas present when she was a teenager, but hasn't owned a cat since (it's said she doesn't really like cats). Currently, the only cat-loving member of the Royal Family is Princess Michael of Kent – who has eight Siamese.

When a Hollywood estate agent overheard the gossip that Burt Reynolds had been homeless and was sharing a house with friends he lost no time in sending Burt details of the luxury houses he had for sale. But he was wasting his time . . . the homeless Burt Reynolds turned out to be a cat, not the actor.

Can first aid be given to an injured cat?

Yes – but always be extremely careful if you are trying to help an injured cat, even your own. Pain and shock can make the friendliest cat bite and struggle. An injured cat will try to crawl away to a quiet place, so probably the best thing you can do if you find one which has been hurt is to place a large cardboard box over it to prevent it disappearing. Telephone a vet and, if you can, enlist the help of an adult.

If an injured cat which is conscious is to be handled, thick gloves should be worn, if possible. A struggling cat can be taken to a vet by wrapping it in a thick jacket. Again, this is easier for an adult to do than a child.

A cat should never be given pain-killers such as aspirin or paracetamol as these are poisonous to cats, and so is alcohol. Don't try home remedy antidotes to poison unless your vet has told you to do so by telephone. And don't put any ointments (or butter) on burns – this will just have to be scraped off again.

Breathing difficulties If a cat has stopped breathing, open its mouth to make sure that nothing is stuck there. Place it on its side with the head stretched out and pull the tongue forward. Place one hand on the ribs and place your other hand on top of it. Press down gently (you could crush its ribs if you apply too much pressure) and release immediately. Do this fifteen times a minute until the cat begins to breathe again on its own.

If a cat has been in water and is unconscious, hold it upside down by the hind legs for about twenty seconds and shake several times to clear the airways of water.

To apply artificial respiration to an unconscious cat, hold

its lips closed and blow gently into its nostrils. Blow until the chest rises then let the animal exhale six to ten times per minute. If it does not, press the chest to expel the air. Take the cat to a vet as soon as possible.

Don't try any of the above methods on a cat which is breathing. If a cat has stopped breathing because it has been electrocuted, do not touch the cat if it is still in contact with the source of electricity – you could be electrocuted too.

Cardiac arrest   If the heart has stopped, place the cat on its side and place your hand on the middle of its chest. Press down *gently* for a count of two and release for a count of one. Repeat sixty times a minute, using artificial respiration (see above) at the same time. Take the cat to a vet as soon as possible.

You can tell the heart has stopped by feeling with your fingertips on the lower part of the chest, or behind the front leg. Or you can listen to the left side of the cat's chest.

Bleeding (external)   Press on the bleeding area using a clean cloth or bandage. In severe cases of injury to a leg or tail, a tourniquet can be applied but must be loosened every five minutes to allow oxygen to the tissues. Loop a bandage or scarf twice around the injured tail or leg above the wound and tie half a knot. Place a short stick on top of the half knot and complete the knot. Twist the stick until the bleeding stops. Take the cat to a vet as soon as possible, remembering to loosen the tourniquet every five minutes.

Burns and scalds   Fill a bucket or bath with cold water and immerse the cat up to the neck for at least five minutes, then take it to a vet. It can be wrapped in wet towels for the journey. Do not remove any blisters or loose skin and do not apply any ointments or anything other than cold water. Ointments will have to be scraped off again before a vet can treat the cat.

Heat stroke   If a cat has been trapped somewhere hot, such as inside a car on a sunny day, it may suffer from heat stroke. Symptoms are rapid breathing and staggering. The tongue, which will be bright red, may be hanging out. In severe cases, immerse the cat in cold water, as above, before taking to a vet. In less severe cases, the cat may improve if it is placed in a cool area.

Shock   A cat will suffer from shock if involved in an accident, as well as having other injuries. Place the cat on its side with its head stretched out in a comfortable place. Check the mouth and throat are clear and pull the tongue forward if the cat is unconscious. Speak soothingly while doing this and keep the cat warm. Take it to a vet as soon as possible.

A cat in shock will have a low temperature, appear confused and weak, have cold feet and may be shivering. The skin will appear pale.

Poisoning   A poisoned cat should be left in a secure, dark place while you telephone a vet. If you know what has caused the poisoning, tell your vet when you telephone. Take the cat to the veterinary surgery as soon as possible.

Symptoms of poisoning include vomiting, diarrhoea, fits and staggering.

Giving a cat pills or medicine   If there is any danger of being bitten, let an adult do this for you! Some cats resist so strongly that they should be restrained by being wrapped in a towel or something similar.

Hold the cat's head with your thumb on one side of the jaw and a finger on the other and tip the head back. The mouth should open. If not, place the nail of a finger of your other hand on the cat's bottom teeth and pull down. Drop the pill right at the back of the cat's mouth. Gently hold the

mouth closed until the cat swallows but make sure you haven't covered the nose with your hand or the cat won't be able to breathe. Stroke the cat's throat to encourage it to swallow.

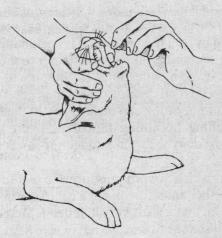

Giving a cat a pill

Liquid medicine is best given by a careful adult as the cat might choke if given too much at a time. If liquid gets into the cat's lungs it can cause damage. Give a few drops at a time by placing the spoon (or dropper) at the side of your cat's mouth, behind the large canine tooth.

If you are still not sure how to give pills or medicine, ask your vet for a demonstration when the medicines are prescribed.

What should I do if my cat eats something poisonous?

Place your cat in a quiet, darkened room while someone telephones a vet for advice. If you know what your cat has been poisoned by, tell the vet and, if it is something which has come in a container, take the container to the telephone to help you answer any questions. It's best *not* to try to make your cat sick as this can do more harm than good.

Symptoms of poisoning can include any of the following: drooling, vomiting, breathing difficulties, depression, muscle tremors, diarrhoea, fits, staggering, loss of consciousness.

Many things which are not poisonous to us and are not poisonous to other animals can kill a cat. Aspirin and paracetamol can make a cat very ill indeed. Medicine for dogs can be poisonous to cats, so never give a cat any medicine unless it has been prescribed for it by a vet. Tobacco and alcohol are poisonous so don't give them to cats (not that I've ever known a cat foolish enough to take either).

Many disinfectants and antiseptics are poisonous to cats. If your cat cuts itself, don't use antiseptic; wash it with warm, salty water. Don't use pine disinfectants around cats, or Dettol, or Jeyes Fluid. The best disinfectant to use is diluted hypochloric acid, which is household bleach. Don't use this on skin and, if using this on floors, don't allow your cat to walk on the floor until it is dry.

If you see a neighbour creosoting a fence, bring your cat indoors until the fence is dry – creosote is also poisonous and your cat may walk on it and then lick its paws. Anti-freeze is poisonous (to dogs as well) yet it has a taste which animals

find pleasant, so make sure your parents and neighbours dispose of old anti-freeze carefully.

Waterproofing or stain-resisting treatments on furniture and carpets can make cats ill, and woodworm treatments can kill. Keep cats out of houses newly treated for woodworm for several weeks, if possible.

In the garden, ask your parents to store fertilisers and bonemeal in lidded containers, not sacks. Insecticides and weedkillers should be used with care, if at all, and cats should not be allowed out until they have dried completely. (If it rains next day or there has been a heavy dew, keep your cat indoors until the ground has dried again.) Slug and snail pellets are also poisonous but can be attractive to cats so they should always be placed under upturned flower pots which have weights on top. Slugs and snails can still get at them, but cats can't.

Many plants are poisonous too, although most cats are too sensible to eat them. However, cats do need to nibble leaves to help their digestion or to help them bring up a hairball, so if you can grow a little grass for them in a tub it might help keep them out of trouble.

Poisonous indoor plants include: dieffenbachias, poinsettias, castor oil plants, azaleas, daffodils, crocuses, hyacinths, chrysanthemums and mistletoe. Spider plants (*Chlorophytum*) are found in most people's homes. Although they are not themselves poisonous, the space agency, NASA, has discovered that they absorb toxins such as carbon monoxide from cigarette smoke or petrol fumes and so can become poisonous.

Poisonous outdoor plants include: daffodils, crocuses, hyacinths, irises, lilies of the valley, chrysanthemums, philodendrons, yew, winter cherry, oleander, Jerusalem cherry, laurel, azaleas, rhododendrons, larkspur, mistletoe,

foxgloves, lupins, laburnum, broom and monkshood.

As you can see, Christmas is a dangerous time for cats as we are more likely then to have mistletoe, poinsettias and possibly spring bulbs growing indoors. Another risk at Christmas time is the needles from a Christmas tree. Although they are not poisonous, a cat can choke on them. It's safer to have an artificial tree. If your tree is real, any needles which drop off should be brushed up regularly.

If you have lots of these plants in your garden, it needn't worry you too much as most cats will leave them alone. But if your parents are buying new plants or shrubs for the garden, it's as easy to buy non-poisonous plants as those which are poisonous.

Interviews

Sarah Greene

'Cous-Cous was our first cat – a tabby with brown markings and a white chin. The colours in his fur reminded us of the meat and rice dish we'd just been enjoying on a holiday in Morocco so we named him Cous-Cous after it!

'He had this great trick every morning to welcome everyone. He'd jump on your shoulder and then circle your head. He could walk around from shoulder to shoulder with no problems at all. He was more like a scarf than a cat.

'Cous-Cous was my particular friend and would sit on my lap while I did my homework. Then we moved from one part of London to another and Cous-Cous didn't like our new home. There were quite a lot of cats around and he may have felt a bit threatened. It was awfully sad – he went away one day and never came back.

'When we moved to the country we got a silver tabby and called him Cous-Cous Two. He was like a little tiger – quite wild – and he loved the countryside. Seven years later we moved back

to London and we didn't think he'd like it there – he was really a country cat. Luckily, the people who bought our house adored him. They wanted to keep him so we left him there where he was happy.

'Now my brother has a tabby cat, identical to Cous-Cous One. Guess what he's called. Cous-Cous Three!'

Phillip Schofield

'My cat story is very sad. It happened at the beginning of the first series of *Going Live!* when my friend's cat had kittens. The cat was a Chinchilla – a very beautiful cat with long white fur tipped with black. The Chinchilla has green eyes with dark rims around them which makes them look as if they are wearing eye-liner! My friend's cat wasn't meant to have kittens – but she had other ideas. She hadn't been spayed, so one day she slipped out and found herself a boyfriend from among the neighbourhood tomcats.

'When the kittens were born, my friend was away from home and his girlfriend telephoned me in a panic. I rushed round to the flat with my little black bag and did what I could to help. Sadly, two of the kittens were born dead and the third was very weak. He was so small he could almost have fitted into an eggcup. Cat mums often reject weak and sickly kittens and that's what happened to this one. His mum refused to look after him or feed him.

'So three human "mums" – me, my friend and his girlfriend –

tried to keep the kitten alive. We sat up all night with him, keeping him warm and feeding him special tinned milk and vitamin supplements. We thought we were winning but when he was five weeks old, he died. It was heartbreaking.

'I really like cats but haven't got one of my own because I'm out working so much. Cats do need company and it wouldn't be fair to keep one if I couldn't spend lots of time with it.'

Simon Hickson

'I really like cats but I can't keep one – I'm allergic to them. I get red, itchy eyes and I start to wheeze. When it's really bad I can't sleep because of asthma.

'It doesn't stop me playing with cats and I still encourage them to come to me. If they're friendly, I like to stuff them up my jumper where they go to sleep! I usually don't get any allergic symptoms at first but, if I keep playing with a cat, after a while I start to wheeze. Then, over a period of time, I get used to the cat and my allergy doesn't bother me so much.

'I once shared a flat with three other students – and Henry. Henry was a very small black cat with white paws. He was great fun . . . completely mad. He spent a lot of his time zooming up the curtains and climbing the walls. Henry slept on the bottom of my bed every night and I found I became used to him. My allergy didn't bother me at all.

'The only thing that bothered me was that Henry would waken up every morning at 6 a.m. and crawl all over my head!'

Trevor Neal

'I've never owned a cat because I have to admit I prefer dogs. I really like mongrels and had a mongrel when I was younger. Now I live in a tower block so I don't think I should keep a cat *or* a dog.

'When I was a kid I used to go round to my friend's house to do my homework and he had a cat I liked a lot. She was a tortoiseshell with only three legs. She'd hurt her leg in an accident and had to have one leg amputated. It didn't slow her down at all. In fact, lots of people didn't even notice she had a missing leg

because she coped brilliantly. I liked her because I thought she was very courageous.

'My only recent contact with cats was when I bought a new guitar case. The owner of the shop owned a kitten and it had been sleeping inside the case which had a cosy fabric lining. Unfortunately, as well as using the case as a bed, it had used it as a toilet! Anyway, it meant I got the case at a reduced price.

'That was months ago and the case still smells dreadful. Does anyone know how to get the smell of cat out of a case?'

Grace McHattie

I've got seven cats at the moment but the number keeps going up. I acquire a new kitten every spring – I can't resist them. Merlin is the oldest – he's a really evil-looking black moggy. He is enormous and very heavy and has huge fangs. The vet hid behind her desk when she saw him for the first time. She didn't need to – he's just a big softy. You only have to look at him and he purrs. He had to have antibiotic tablets recently (he'd been fighting, as usual) and he crunched them up like sweeties. Morgan is another black moggy and she is very sweet – except if you move a muscle when she's sitting on your lap.

I have four Ragdolls at the moment. These are cats which came from California and there aren't many of them in the United Kingdom yet. Crystal is very beautiful. She has long, blonde fur with bright blue eyes. She looks as if she is wearing long brown velvet gloves and a velvet mask. She was the first guest ever to appear on *Going Live!* Andy is very sweet-natured and pretty. She's female so her name confuses everyone – it's short for Superstar Andromeda. I've also got a Superstar Betelgeuse – BeeJay for short, who is very young and very greedy and very noisy.

Mighty Mouse is my male Ragdoll, so called because he is rather small for his age and he doesn't miaow – he squeaks just like a mouse. Squirt is my Devon Rex. Squirt doesn't like the Ragdolls at all and punches them in the face when I'm not looking.

Like Simon, I'm allergic to cats. Is there any type of cat I can keep?

If you're allergic to cats, it really is best not to keep a cat at all. Cat allergies can be caused by a number of things; you may be allergic to the cat's fur, or to its saliva, or to the tiny flakes of skin which rub off on to the fur. Even the Sphynx, a cat with almost no fur, can cause a reaction in someone who is allergic to its saliva or skin. Rex cats have very short fur so some allergy sufferers have bought them hoping that they will not be allergic to them. In many cases, the allergy has continued and the unfortunate cats have had to be rehomed.

What happens if you already have a cat and you become allergic to it? If your allergy is very mild and you don't want to find another home for your cat, there are some things you can do to ease the problem:

- Have someone groom your cat daily so there are no loose hairs coming off its coat.
- Have your cat bathed regularly, if it doesn't object too strenuously.
- Have someone else empty litter trays. If you have to do it, wear a dust mask from a DIY store.
- Smooth, washable surfaces are easier to keep fur-free. Vinyl is better than carpets and blinds are better than curtains. All surfaces should be wiped over regularly with a damp cloth.
- An air purifier might help.
- There are also desensitising injections available but these are not suitable for everyone. Your doctor will advise you about them.

If you are seriously allergic to cats, you might consider

'adopting' one instead of owning one. Most cat rescue shelters have cats which they cannot rehome because they are too nervous or too old or they are just unwanted. These cats will live all their lives in the shelters and many are supported by cat-lovers who 'adopt' them but who are, for many different reasons, unable to give a home to a cat. For a small monthly sum, you will be kept informed of the progress of 'your' cat and you may even receive a card at Christmas.

There's another side to the allergy story. Many *cats* suffer from allergies too – although, fortunately, I've never heard of one who was allergic to its owner!

Many cats are allergic to milk, some are allergic to certain types of tinned cat food, a few are even allergic to red meat and live on fish and chicken. Cat litter can occasionally cause problems, especially if it is very dusty or if deodorant has been added.

Many other things can cause allergic reactions in cats, including carpet cleaners or other household cleansers, pollen, fleas, plastic bowls, perfume and cigarette smoke.

Symptoms of allergy vary and include runny eyes, sneezing, coughing, diarrhoea, vomiting and bald patches.

My cat wets on the carpets and furniture. How can I stop this?

There are many reasons why a cat soils where it shouldn't – and it is never done out of spite or revenge, as some owners believe. A cat may urinate or defecate where it shouldn't, squatting down to do so. Or it may spray, in which case urine is sprayed backwards onto a vertical surface while the cat stands upright with its back to the object being sprayed.

Urinating or defaecating in the wrong place may be a sign of an **illness**, some of which are very serious, even life-threatening. This may be the only way a cat has to show its owners that something is wrong, so a soiling cat should first be taken to a vet for a check-up. If illness is not the cause, it may be any of the following:

Stress   Cats are creatures of habit and hate it when anything changes. They can be stressed by a change of home, someone leaving the household, someone joining (human or pet), by their owners going on holiday or by the cat having an accident or illness which may necessitate wearing a bandage or splint, or being restrained in some other way.

Confusion   Cats usually cover up what is in their litter trays. Some cats do this with their paws outside their trays and then confuse the carpet (if that is what they feel under their paws) with their litter. They then soil the carpet the next time. Prevent this by placing the litter tray inside a larger cardboard box or on a large sheet of plastic.

No litter tray   Two-thirds of all cat owners still don't provide their cats with a tray for indoor use – then wonder

why they have problems! Cats simply won't go out of doors on a stormy night with wind and rain whipping around them while they squat down on a patch of wet mud. Can you blame them?

Dislike of the litter or tray   Some cats prefer one type of litter to another. Some litters have deodorant added and many cats will not use this. Cats won't use a dirty tray or one another cat has used (would you use a dirty toilet?). And if the tray is clean, the smell of the disinfectant used may be putting the cat off. Wash litter trays in a diluted solution of household bleach.

Old age or hormones   Old cats don't have the same control over their muscles as they did when they were younger. They should be provided with an upstairs tray and a downstairs tray if you live in a house, as they may not have time to get to the tray if there is only one. And female cats, when they are ready to be mated, will frequently urinate on carpets or furniture. Neutering stops this.

Allergy   A few cats become allergic to their food, even if it is tinned food which doesn't affect other cats. So if your cat begins to soil, try changing its food to see if there is an improvement.

Territorial marking   This is a common reason for soiling and *the* most common reason for spraying. Each cat has its own territory, indoors and out of doors, and only has one way of marking it – urinating on it. This horrifies many owners but the cats simply don't understand why their owners are angry. What the cat is doing is the same as if you wrote your name in a book – you are saying it is yours. Cats can't write, or erect fences or signs, so they have to urinate on their territory to point out to other cats that it *is* theirs. If

you were told off for writing your name in a book and told you were dirty, you wouldn't understand at all. Neither does a cat which is marking its territory. Being cross with your cat simply puts it under more stress and the problem could get worse. So try to understand why your cat is marking its territory in this way. If it is because a new cat has come into your household, give your cat its own space – perhaps somewhere to sleep away from the other cat. Be patient and spend time with your cat, so that it knows you still care for it. The problem may cease when it no longer feels threatened.

Spraying can also be caused by **stress** (see above), because your cat **is not neutered** (neutered cats spray much less frequently than those which have not been neutered), or because a **female** cat in the area is ready for mating (this can make even a neutered cat spray). Contrary to popular belief, both male and female cats spray, although females are less likely to.

Cats stropping (sharpening their claws) on the furniture is another problem that parents don't appreciate at all. If your cat does so, it must be provided with a scratching post. Take your cat away from the furniture, saying 'no' in a loud, firm voice, and place your cat by the scratching post. If necessary, demonstrate how your cat should use it. If a cat sees someone scratching a post, it is often encouraged to do the same. You must tell your cat off each time it scratches the furniture and, if it isn't getting the message, cover the part of the furniture which is being scratched with plastic sheeting. Cats hate the feel of plastic under their paws and won't scratch it.

In fact, plastic sheeting is a wonderful substance for covering any object you don't want your cat to soil on, scratch, or otherwise mess up. The problem is that you can end up with rather a lot of it spread throughout your home!

Legends

How the Manx cat lost its tail

When Noah filled the Ark, the animals trooped in two by two – all except the Manx cats which were having too much fun to go inside. They gambolled and played and ignored Noah when he called them to hurry. Noah told them that he had to shut the doors soon – but they paid no attention.

Then it began to rain – harder and harder. They heard the great door creak as it began to close and they rushed for the doorway, frightened that they would be too late and would be left to drown.

Just as the door closed, they managed to dash inside – but their tails were trapped in the door. Ever since, the Manx has been the cat without a tail – cut off by the doors of Noah's Ark.

The legend of the Birman

The Birman is also known as the Sacred Cat of Burma and was said to have belonged to the temple priests hundreds of years ago. The priests of western Burma worshipped a golden, blue-eyed goddess called Tsun-Kyan-Kse. They kept 100 white cats in their temple because they believed that, when one of the 100 priests died, his soul would enter one of the cats and so live on.

Then, one night as the chief priest prayed at the temple of the goddess, bandits stormed the temple and attacked him.

One of the cats, grief-stricken at the sight of the mortally wounded priest, placed his paws on the chief priest's head – and a miracle occurred. As the priest died, the cat turned golden like the goddess. His yellow eyes turned blue, like the goddess's eyes. His face, ears, legs and tail darkened and became the colour of the earth on which the priest lay – but his paws remained white as a symbol of purity.

The beautiful cat inspired the remaining priests to fight back and repel the bandits. Then they discovered that all of the 100 cats in the temple had become the beautifully-coloured cats they are today; coloured like Siamese but with long hair.

Names to call your cat

Every time I meet a scratched and battered old tom cat with
ripped ears, a body covered in scars and maybe even a missing
eye, I discover his name is Lucky. And every time I meet a
Rambo, I am introduced to a small and puny kitten which runs
away at the sight of its own shadow. Cat names are very difficult
to choose because what suits a kitten may not suit the cat it
grows into. Another difficulty is that some names become very
dated; if you meet a cat called ET, for example, you know that it is
at least six or seven years old! Anyway, here to help you choose a
name for your cat or kitten are a few suggestions, as well as the
most popular cats' names in the United Kingdom.

Cat names top thirty

Sooty	Lucky	Tabby	Timmy	Muffin
Tiger	Suzie	Sam	Puss	Tinker
Smokey	Fluffy	Tiddles	Penny	Tibby
Tigger	Snowy	Tabitha	Fluff	Topsy
Whiskey	Suky	Blackie	Charlie	Tom
Kitty	Thomas	Ginger	Misty	Cleo

(*Source:* Kattomeat/Gallup survey)

Names to call your cat

Abracadabra	name for a magic cat
Ace	name for an absolutely brilliant cat
Allegro	music with a fast tempo (also a type of car)
Angelica	a little angel or a type of candied plant
Asparagus	one of the *Cats* cats. *Spargel* is the German word for asparagus and is a nice name too
AWOL	stands for Absent Without Leave
Baba	cake flavoured with rum, usually circular in shape
Bacardi	white rum
Bagel	a round bread roll
Balalaika	Russian musical instrument
Bandido	Spanish for 'bandit'
Bangles	tabby cats often have bangle markings around their legs
Banjo	stringed musical instrument
Barnacle	shellfish which attaches itself to rocks; good name for a crusty (or shellfish) cat
Basil	a herb; also Latin for 'kingly'
Beardsley	after the artist famous for black and white prints; therefore a good name for a black and white cat
Bianca	white
Biscuit	name for a biscuit-coloured (or crumby) cat
Blanche	French for 'white'
Blimp	an airship, so a good name for a fat cat
Bo	Chinese for 'precious'
Bobbin	a spool for holding thread
Bogey	a naughty imp – also actor Humphrey Bogart's nickname
Bongo	a type of antelope – might suit a fast cat
Bonita	Spanish for 'pretty'
Bonny, Bonnie	Scots for 'pretty'
Boots	name for a cat with white feet
Bovril	black cat name if you don't mind advertising

Boyero	Spanish for 'cowboy'
Burrito	Mexican food
Butterscotch	very hard brown sweet
Buttons	for owners who like Cinderella or a name for cats with spots
Calico	cotton cloth and, in the USA, the name given to a tortoiseshell and white cat
Calypso	melodic West Indian song
Cannonball	could suit a cat which is either very round, very fast or very destructive!
Cara	Italian for 'dear one'
Caraway	strong tasting seed used in baking
Carnegie	very wealthy American
Cassandra	one of the *Cats* cats
Chanterelle	a type of mushroom
Chen	Chinese for 'great'
Cheshire	the grinning cat in *Alice in Wonderland*
Christie	a ski-ing turn
Chutney	a way of preserving fruit or vegetables. Nice name for a cat which is a bit of a mixture
Cleopatra	queen of the Nile
Crumpet	a sort of pancake with holes
Daffy	name of a cartoon duck and also means riding two skateboards at once
Diablo	Spanish for 'devil'
Dino	Fred Flintstone's pet dinosaur
Domino	name for a black cat with white spot(s)
Dumpling	another fat cat name!
Ebony	black wood
Felix	Latin for 'cat'; also means lucky
Fergie	name for a red-haired cat (or *Duchess* or *Yorkie*)
Filigree	this is ornamental wirework, so would be a good name for an intricately-patterned cat
Finnan	terrific Scottish name for a red cat. A Finnan Haddie is a smoked haddock
Flynn	Gaelic for 'red-haired'

Fudge	name for a gingery-brown cat
Galoshes	American word for waterproof overshoes
Garbo	actress who wanted to be alone
Garçon	French for waiter. Ideal for the cat with a black dinner jacket and a white shirtfront
Garnet	semi-precious stone
Gingerbread	a type of biscuit
Gingersnap	snap!
Gordon Blue	for a blue (grey) cat
Goulash	posh name for stew. Good name for a cat of mixed ancestry
Growltiger	one of the *Cats* cats
Guinness	Irish stout drink, black underneath and white on top
Gumdrop	a sweet
Guzzle	a hearty eater
Harlequin	a bit of a clown
Harvey	Harvey appeared (or did he?) in an old James Stewart film. He was a six-foot-high invisible rabbit
Hoopla	game where rings are thrown over prizes
Houdini	famous escape artist
Jasper	semi-precious stone
Jet	semi-precious stone
Johnson	Samuel Johnson, famous compiler of dictionaries, bought oysters personally for his cat in case his servants came to dislike the feline because of this extra chore
Jumble	a mixed-up cat
Keiller	a famous marmalade
Kelly	Gaelic for 'brave warrior'
Kirk	from *Star Trek*. A name for cats which boldly go . . .
Knödel	pronounce the 'ö' as if you are running an 'o' and an 'e' together to make an 'eu' sound – a *Knödel* is a German dumpling
Kopek	Russian small change

69

Koto	Japanese stringed instrument
Layla	Arabic for 'night'
Leo	Latin for 'lion'; a sign of the zodiac
Lucifer	a devil
Macaroon	small, round almond cake
Macavity	one of the *Cats* cats
Magnum	a very large wine bottle and Tom Selleck's television character. Either way the name would suit a very large cat
Marigold	a golden flower
Marmalade	sticky-sounding name suits ginger cats
Medley	a miscellaneous collection of things
Merle	French for 'blackbird'
Merlin	magical teacher of King Arthur. Great name for black cats with a white star or moon under their chin
Midnight	name for an all-black cat
Mittens	gloves with no fingers ('You've lost your mittens, you naughty kittens'.)
Mongo	an evil planet in *Flash Gordon*
Mosaic	a patchwork – usually made of tiles
Mulligan	a sort of stew
Mushroom	the name of my cousin's tabby cat
Nutmeg	a brown spice, good with custard
Nyan Nyan	pronounce the 'yan' like 'ian' in 'piano'. Japanese for 'kitten'
O'Malley	singing cat in *The Aristocats* film
Pacco	Italian for 'parcel'
Paprika	a hot, red spice
Patches	name for a cat of many colours
Pfennig	pronounce it fennik. It's a German penny
Picasso	name for a blue (grey) cat. Picasso was a famous artist who had a blue period, when he painted many paintings with the colour blue
Pierrot	a black and white clown
Popcorn	a bouncy cat

70

Pudding	some cats simply *are* Puddings. If you've got one, you'll know
Puffball	it's a round toadstool but it sounds nice!
Pumpernickel	black bread
Pumpkin	a large, round vegetable but also, believe it or not, a term of endearment in North America
Pyewacket	very ancient cat's name; especially one belonging to a witch
Rhubarb	might be a good name for a cat which is very talkative
Rick O'Shea	name for a cat which cannons around the room
Rojo	pronounce the 'o's as in rock and the 'j' as an 'h'. It's Spanish for 'red'
Rufus	ancient name for someone with red hair
Rum Tum Tugger	another one of the *Cats* cats
Rusty	for cats which shouldn't be left out in the rain
Sacré Bleu	French swear word. Good name for a naughty blue (grey) cat
Sarge	short for sergeant; sergeants have stripes
Scooter	name for a cat which scoots around the house
Shannon	Gaelic for 'little wise man'
Shere Khan	*The Jungle Book* tiger
Sherry	a good name for a cat of that colour
Smirnoff	a Russian vodka
Smog	a thick, grey cat?
Snowball	white cat names
Snowdrop	
Snowflake	
Snowy	
Solitaire	a game for one person to play on their own
Sou	French small change. A good name for girl cats but don't have a boy named Sou . . .
Spock	from *Star Trek*. Either a pointed-eared cat or one with a very logical mind . . .
Spritzer	a drink of wine and soda

Sushi	Japanese raw fish dish
Taffeta	a lightweight dress fabric
Tamale	pronounce it Ta-ma-lee – it's a Mexican pancake
Tao	the name of the Siamese in *The Incredible Journey*
Tapioca	a gooey pudding
Tiger Lily	flower; usually orange and striped
TNT	Tri-Nitro-Toluene – a powerful explosive
Tortilla	pronounce it Tor-tee-ya – it's a sort of hard Mexican pancake
Tuxedo	American word for dinner jacket
Vashti	Persian for 'beautiful'
Velvet	name for a cat with soft fur
Weeny	for a little cat (but beware, small cats often grow into big cats)
Winkie	after Wee Willie – might suit a cat which sleeps a lot

Twos and threes

Adam and Eve
Ann and Andy
Bacon and Eggs
Barnum and Bailey
Bonnie and Clyde
Brandy and Soda
Bubble and Squeak
Cider with Rosie
Gin and Tonic
Ham and Eggs
Jack and Jill
Laurel and Hardy
Loco and Motion
Marks and Spencer

Mork and Mindy
Nutmeg and Custard
Pork and Beans
Salt and Pepper
Simon and Garfunkel
Tom and Jerry
Whisky and Soda
Faith, Hope and Charity
Lock, Stock and Barrel
Louie, Dewey and Huey
Snap, Crackle and Pop
Tom, Dick and Harry
Yum-Yum, Peep-Bo and Pitti-Sing

Cat games

The Minister's Cat

I have no idea why this game is called the Minister's Cat – it could just as easily be called the Bricklayer's Cat. Whatever you call it, it can be played by two or more.

Take it in turns to say, 'The Minister's Cat is a .... cat,' filling in the blank with a word beginning with 'a'. For example, you could say, 'The Minister's Cat is an active cat.' The next person might say, 'The Minister's Cat is an Angora cat,' and so on.

The adjectives don't have to make sense, in fact it's more fun if they don't. You could say, 'The Minister's Cat is an antiseptic cat' or ' . . . an artistic cat'. When you run out of words beginning with 'a', go on to 'b', then 'c' and on through the alphabet.

Poor Pussy

This is a game to see who can keep a straight face longest. Two or more can play.

One player becomes the 'Poor Pussy' and must get on hands and knees. Pussy then crawls over to another player and miaows three times. This player must say 'Poor Pussy' and stroke the pussy's head *without laughing, smiling or giggling*. If the player keeps a straight face, they become the pussy. If they don't, they are out of the game. The winner is the last player left in the game. The pussy is allowed to cheat by giggling as well as miaowing.

Cat and Canary

This game requires at least three or four players. One player should be blindfolded and have a 'canary' in front of him or her. The canary can be any object; an old sock makes a good one. The other players are the cats and they should sit several feet away from the blindfolded player.

One of the cats creeps forward to try to steal the canary and take it back to their place, without the blindfolded player hearing them. If the cat succeeds, he or she changes places with the blindfolded player.

Cats don't need any help from us when they're having kittens, do they?

When cats which live wild give birth, they are often helped by other queens (female cats) which act as midwives, helping them clean up the kittens as they are born. Most cats living in human families like to have this sort of help from their owners. Some cats, if their humans are out, will not give birth until the owners return and are able to help them. And many cats become upset if their owners leave the room before they've given birth to their last kitten.

So cats do like company when giving birth and they do sometimes need help. Veterinary assistance is occasionally needed with a difficult birth.

It is much easier to help the cat if she has a convenient 'nest' in which to give birth. Left to their own devices, cats will find warm, dark, secure places to give birth – for example, in the airing cupboard. This makes it very difficult for anyone trying to help, so provide her with a suitable nest in a place which can easily be reached. A large, clean cardboard carton is ideal. Use one which has held a product which doesn't smell, such as cornflakes or potato crisps.

Another large carton can be placed upside down over the first, with corresponding holes cut in the side. The top box can be lifted off while help is given at the birth and then replaced to make a dark nest for cat and kittens to sleep in. Line the box with many layers of newspaper for warmth and place strips of kitchen towel on top. This should be changed after the birth and then changed at least once a day.

The first indication that a queen is about to give birth may be when she goes into her kittening box. Or she may seem restless, unable to settle, or begin to pant or purr. There may be a clear discharge from the vulva (the opening just in front of the anus) or a spot of blood. Make sure that the kittening room is very warm and quiet. Don't allow lots of people to witness the birth; the cat will only want the company of one or two people she knows well.

The cat's muscles will begin to contract in order to push out a kitten and these contractions can last a few minutes to thirty minutes or more. If they last longer than sixty to ninety minutes without producing a kitten, contact your vet.

As the kittens are born, the cat may deal with them herself or may leave them for her owner to look after. A kitten arrives in a nice, neat bag, called a birth sac, which is attached to a placenta by the umbilical cord. The placenta has provided all the nourishment the kitten has needed before it was born. The kittens should be removed from their birth sacs as soon as possible. The sacs are very fragile and can easily be torn open with the fingers. The umbilical cord can be left intact while the kitten's nose and mouth are wiped clean and the kitten is rubbed dry with a towel. Mum may show interest again at this stage and should be allowed to lick the kitten dry if she wishes. The umbilical cord can then be carefully cut if the cat hasn't dealt with this. A piece of thread should be tied around the cord 4–5 cm from the

kitten's abdomen (tummy). Cut the cord on the same side as the placenta using sterilised, blunt-ended scissors.

Place the kitten at its mother's teats. A healthy kitten will immediately begin trying to suckle. The kittens must be kept warm and out of draughts. Their mother will usually curl around them to keep them warm. If one becomes cold, it should be immersed up to the neck in hand-warm water.

Count the placentas to make sure there is one for every kitten. If not, you must contact your vet immediately as a placenta remaining inside the cat will cause a serious infection which could kill her. The placentas may appear almost immediately as the kittens are born, or they may take half an hour or more. Don't pull them; allow them to appear in their own time. The queen may eat the placentas and it is thought they help start her milk flow. Allow her to eat one or two but remove the rest as they can cause a stomach upset.

Most cats manage all the chores of kittening very well by themselves. Don't 'help' (or interfere) unless it is necessary.

Call your vet immediately if:

- the cat strains for more than an hour without producing a kitten
- there is more than three hours between kittens
- the cat seems distressed
- she passes a yellow or green discharge, or more than a spot of blood, before the kittens are born
- there is blood or any other discharge after the kittens are born
- the cat appears to be going into labour early (before nine weeks)
- you are worried about her in any way

If the cat is unable to feed her kittens, they will have to be hand-reared with a milk substitute which you can buy from

Cutting the umbilical cord

pet stores and vets. Small animal feeding bottles can also be bought there, or a clean eye dropper can be used. Don't feed kittens cows' milk, as it doesn't contain enough protein. New-born kittens have to be fed at two-hourly intervals, day and night. After each feed, their tummies must be rubbed and their bottoms wiped until they eliminate any waste. They aren't able to do this for themselves for four weeks and usually their mother does it for them by licking them.

Keep all visitors away from kittens for the first few weeks. Too many visitors can upset mum and, if she is disturbed, she may try to move the kittens to a quieter place. Cats move kittens by holding them by the scruff of the neck in their mouths. This is the only way they can carry kittens (because they have no hands) but it is not ideal. An inexperienced mum may cut the kitten's skin with her teeth or accidentally bang the kitten against furniture or even pick the kitten up wrongly – by the leg, for example. So, although mum and kittens should be checked daily by one person to see that they are healthy and the kittens are thriving, they should otherwise be left in peace so that mum doesn't feel that she has to move her kittens.

And if *you* are picking up kittens, wash your hands thoroughly first. Infections can be passed on very easily to young kittens. When you pick them up, do so by placing one hand under their bottoms and one around their back or chest, supporting them. Never pick them up by the scruff of the neck – it places a lot of strain on their neck muscles. Of course, your friends will be very keen to see your kittens. Tell them they can do so when the kittens are three or four weeks old. They must wash their hands if they want to touch the kittens, although ideally they shouldn't touch the kittens at all if they have a cat of their own.

It's up to the cat's owners to keep her and her kittens safe for the first weeks of their lives. Make sure that no tomcats can get into your home; if they do they will kill the kittens. So cat flaps and windows should be kept closed. Mum can start calling again – and is ready to mate – within a month of giving birth, so she should be kept indoors so that she doesn't become pregnant again. She can become pregnant while she is still feeding her kittens and, as well as adding to the total of unwanted kittens in the world, such a short time between pregnancies will damage her health.

It really is kinder to have her spayed. It would have been even kinder to have had her spayed at the age of four to six months – then she wouldn't have had to go through the hard work of pregnancy and the pain of kittenbirth!

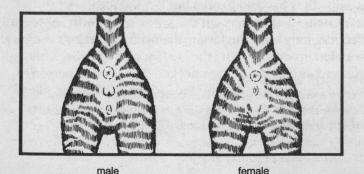

male   female

Cat expressions

No room to swing a cat
This doesn't refer to a feline but to a cat o' nine tails – a type of whip with nine thongs used as a form of punishment 200 years ago in the English navy. Because a cat o' nine tails was much smaller than an ordinary whip, any space too small to swing one was small indeed!

Grin like a Cheshire cat
This expression probably started life as 'grin like a *cheeser* cat'. Cats in cheese-making areas were often given pieces of cheese to eat as a treat. Most cats adore cheese (it *is* made from milk) and would look so pleased with themselves they almost grinned. The corruption from cheeser to Cheshire is appropriate; Cheshire produces a delicious cheese of its own. This cheese may, at one time, have had a grinning cat stamped on its end – a Cheshire cat.

Let the cat out of the bag
In the last century, country folk would sell their goods at market. Some were not as honest as they might have been and many tricks were played. One trick was to try to sell 'a pig in a poke', a pig in a bag. The seller would try to persuade a buyer to purchase his pig in a poke without opening the bag to check it out (probably after the buyer had had a few pints of beer or cider). Often, there wouldn't be a porker inside; instead of a piglet, there would be a cat, which was much less valuable. Any buyer who kept his wits about him would insist on inspecting the merchandise and would open the bag, whereupon the cat would, of course, run away. Now 'letting the cat out of the bag' means to give away a secret.

In the dark all cats are grey
This means that everyone is basically alike but that it is only obvious under certain circumstances. However, the proverb doesn't seem to make much sense. All cats are *not* grey in the dark – to us. But a cat's colour vision is poor in the dark so *to a cat* all other cats probably are grey at night.

It's raining cats and dogs

Meaning that it is raining very heavily, this expression may have come from the Greek word for waterfall, *catadupa*, which became changed to 'cats and dogs' over the centuries.

Cats love fish but fear to wet their paws

This is said when someone wants something badly but won't take any trouble to achieve it. In fact, cats usually prefer meat to fish – especially if they have to catch the fish themselves.

Cats have nine lives

They don't – but they show an amazing ability to survive in difficult circumstances.

I'll do it before the cat can lick its ear

This means never – because a cat can't lick its ear.

A cat may look at a king

Anyone, no matter how humble, is just as good as the highest in the land.

Curiosity killed the cat

Cats are extremely curious and consequently get into danger when exploring new things.

Playing cat and mouse

This means to toy with someone, unkindly catching them just to let them go and catch them again. Although cats appear to be cruel when catching mice or other small creatures, they are not. It's simply that their interest in hunting is triggered by movement; when a mouse 'plays dead' the cat loses interest and its interest only revives when the mouse begins to move again.

Catnap

Meaning to have a short sleep. Cats sleep sixteen hours a day or more but will wake instantly if they sense danger – or food!

Fighting like cat and dog

This means a fierce fight. But if cats and dogs have been properly introduced, they won't fight at all.

My cat dribbles and kneads my skin with its paws when it's happy. Why?

When a kitten is new-born, there is only one pleasurable experience in its life – being fed. As it suckles from its mother, it kneads either side of her teat. This makes the milk flow more quickly. So, in later life, when some cats are feeling good, they knead as they did at that happy time. They also dribble because their mouths water as they did when they were enjoying their mother's milk. Kneading is a happy thing for your cat to do and it simply won't understand that it might be hurting you, so it is pretty well impossible to stop. All you can do if your cat is a kneader (not all are) is to trim a little off its claws to blunt them (see page 36) and wear thick trousers!

It's easy to tell how your cat is feeling just by watching its behaviour. Kneading is one way of telling if your cat is happy. Another is if your cat walks tall with its ears held high and its tail sticking straight up in the air. If its tail is bent over at the tip, it's even happier. Tails say a lot about how a cat is feeling. A tail carried stiff and low tells you that a cat is cautious. A tail which is drooping sideways shows a lack of interest in whatever is going on at the time. A tail slowly

wagging from side to side shows that a cat is alert – and may become annoyed – at which time the tail will thrash wildly from side to side. The hairs on the tail can stand on end, so a cat facing another in a fight situation might have a tail which looks like a bottle-brush. It helps make the cat look bigger and more of a threat to the other.

Ears and eyes indicate mood too. Upright ears show happiness and contentment. If you stroke a cat whose ears are upright, the ears may swivel slightly sideways, to show that your stroking is making the cat even happier. A cat will flatten its ears against its head if a fight threatens, to protect them from damage, as fighting cats swipe at one another's heads with their claws. A cat will blink slowly and deliberately at another cat (or sometimes even a person) to show that they pose no threat and want to be friends. If you blink at your cat and it blinks back, this is said to be the cat equivalent of a kiss. Blinking is the opposite signal to the stare which, in the cat world, is a threat. Two cats which are about to fight will stare hard at one another. Often, if you place a newspaper or magazine between them, so they can no longer see one another, they'll forget about having a fight and go off in different directions!

This is the key to make friends with a cat. If we like cats and meet a new cat, we always stare at it. What we don't realise is that we are threatening the cat by staring at it. What we should do is enter the room where the cat is and completely ignore it. If you can't resist looking at it, you should blink frequently and slowly. Of course, people who don't like cats don't look at them – which is why cats always go to people who don't like them. (All they have to do to stop cats bothering them is to stare at them when they first meet and the cats won't go anywhere near them.)

Whiskers move according to a cat's mood. If a cat is

looking forward to something (for example, if it sees its food being prepared) its whiskers will point forward. In a fight, the whiskers will be drawn back as the teeth are bared, emphasising the snarl.

An anxious or nervous cat will lick its lips rapidly. This can be seen in any vet's waiting room! A very nervous cat will 'flehm', gasping and inhaling air through its slightly-open mouth. Cats have a unique organ in the roofs of their mouths which allows them to taste and smell at the same time. Cats can literally taste the air and learn much from it. So a cat will flehm in response to something new in the environment as well as when anxious or when danger threatens.

Yawning is a sign of reassurance in the cat world (as well as a sign that a cat feels sleepy). So if you want to make friends with a cat, get down to its level so that you are not towering over it, yawn frequently and blink slowly, while talking in a quiet, calm voice. It may look very odd, but you'll make a friend for life!

Strange but true

Chinese peasants believed they could tell the time by looking at a cat's eyes. According to them, a cat's pupils are widest in the morning and afternoon and narrowest at noon.

A black and white American cat called Princess Kitty can do thirty tricks such as shaking paws, sitting up and begging and playing basketball on a scaled-down court. She can also play *Three Blind Mice* on a piano. In 19th-century Italy, a circus showman called Pietro Capelli taught his troupe of cats to play musical instruments, walk tightropes, swing from trapezes and juggle balls with their hind legs. Pietro spoke three languages and his cats could understand instructions given in all three.

Strange but true . . .

In a year, the average cat will eat twenty-seven times its own weight in food, getting through nearly 130 000 calories. It needs three times as many calories, weight for weight, as its owner. The year's calories will be made up of 280 tins of cat food, fifteen packets of dry cat food and 23 kilos of fresh meat and fish. It has been estimated that it costs around £5000 to care for a cat during an average fourteen-year lifespan.

Calvin Coolidge came from humble beginnings to become President of the United States of America. He held a formal dinner at the White House to which some of his relatives were invited. They were unsure about how to behave at such a fancy affair, so they copied everything he did. This worked out fine until coffee was served. When the President poured half his coffee into his saucer, his guests copied him. He then added milk and sugar to the coffee in the saucer. His guests followed suit. Then the President put his saucer on the floor . . . for his cat.

Robinson Crusoe's 'Man Friday' was probably a cat. Robinson Crusoe was really called Alexander Selkirk and was a mariner who was put ashore on an uninhabited island as a punishment for mutiny. There were rats and wild cats on the island and, while he slept, the rats would often gnaw his feet. So he made friends with the cats by feeding them fish he had caught and they slept around him, protecting him from the rats. But he had nightmares about the cats, thinking that, when he died, they would eat his body! They didn't – Alexander Selkirk was rescued from his island after four years and four months.

I'm buying a kitten to keep my cat company. How should I introduce them?

Introducing a new cat or kitten can take some time but, if it is done properly, the animals will get on better together than if they are just thrown together. Cats can become very jealous and may sulk if a new kitten arrives – or even run away from home! Prevent this sort of problem by introducing them carefully.

You may find it is a good idea to quarantine your new kitten for a few days, to make sure it is completely healthy and won't pass on any illnesses to your cat. Kittens can pick up infections very easily but it may take a few days before the symptoms are seen. So, particularly if your kitten came from a source you aren't sure of, you should keep it separate from your cat for a few days if you can.

Keep it in a room with somewhere cosy to sleep, its own litter tray and food and water bowls. Obviously, if it is left entirely alone it will be very lonely and unhappy, so try to spend as much time with it as possible. Kittens sleep for as much as twenty hours a day, so you won't have to spend all day in one room. When you leave its room, wash your hands before touching your cat and, ideally, you should change your clothes too, as infection (should your kitten have one) can be passed on by touch.

Your cat will know that there is a new feline being kept separately and will sniff at the doorway. It will become used to the smell of the kitten before it sees it. After five or six days you can introduce the two, if you are sure both are quite healthy. If you haven't quarantined your kitten, start the introduction process from here.

85

Trim your cat's and kitten's claws (see page 36). If they do fight, they will do one another less damage with blunted claws. Decide in which room you will introduce them and make sure there are plenty of hiding places there for your kitten. If there aren't, put down some empty cardboard boxes for your kitten to run into if the going gets rough.

There's only one difficult bit in introductions and this is it. *You must completely ignore the kitten until your cat has made friends with it.*

Even if your cat biffs the kitten on the ear – and it will – you must not rush over and separate them. Your cat has something very important to teach your kitten – that your cat is the boss. Once the kitten understands this, the two can be friends. If you interrupt the lesson your cat is teaching the kitten, both may become confused and resentful.

There may be a lot of horrible noises – spitting, hissing, growling and wailing. There will be fighting, tumbling, biting and slashing. *Let them get on with it.* Your cat really is just asserting itself and has no intention of hurting your kitten. Kittens are rarely, if ever, hurt by adult cats, once they are weaned. They are smart little creatures and they soon learn to make themselves look small and unthreatening. If it gets a bit too rough they know to withdraw and hide under the sofa or in a cardboard box.

You might separate them at night, or if you are going out, for the first day or two, until you feel sure they are getting on well together.

They must have separate beds at first. They will decide when, or if, they want to sleep together. They must also be fed from separate bowls and these should be placed several metres apart, as strange felines don't like eating close together. As they become friends, you can place the bowls closer together. If, during the time they are being introduced, you feed them, this will probably take their minds off one another – as long as they are fed at some distance from each other.

If you are introducing a new adult cat to your cat, it should be done in the same way. Kittens settle down in a new home within a day or two, but it may take longer for an adult cat to settle down. Some will settle in hours, while others take weeks or months. It really depends on the cat.

If you have bought a puppy or dog and want to introduce it to your cat, ensure it is under control on a leash and that you make it understand it is not to chase your cat. Many dogs and cats live together and get on extremely well; however, the same dog may enjoy chasing other people's cats although it wouldn't dream of touching its 'own' cat.

I don't believe cats should be introduced to small pets,

rodents, birds or insects. These creatures would provide food for a cat living wild and your cat's instincts may overcome its friendly nature. I know there are a few cats which have budgie or mouse 'friends' but it is really expecting too much of a cat to be pals with its lunch. Remember, too, that rabbits, despite their larger size, are the natural prey of many cats. If you keep a rabbit and a cat, always keep them apart. Otherwise you may come home from school one day to find your rabbit with its feet in the air and your cat looking smug.

Superstitions

There are more superstitions connected with cats than with any other animal. And more superstitions involve black cats than any other colour. This may be because cats were once considered to be the 'familiars' of witches – spirits or devils in furry form. Black has long been considered the colour of evil.

Yet in the United Kingdom, black cats are considered to be lucky, especially if they cross your path. In some areas of the country it's believed you must stroke a black cat three times for luck. Bad luck will follow if a black cat runs away from you. Good fortune is certain if a black cat enters a house uninvited, as long as the cat isn't chased away. If it is, it will take all the luck of the house with it.

In Yorkshire in the last century it was believed that keeping a black cat in a sailor's house meant that he would never drown. So popular was the black cat in coastal areas that they were frequently stolen! And a black cat aboard ship, especially one with no white hairs, was considered very lucky. Hundreds of years ago it was thought that if a girl kept a black cat, she would always have lots of boyfriends. In parts of Yorkshire it is thought to be lucky to own a black cat, but unlucky to meet one.

Yet in the USA and many parts of Europe, black cats are considered *un*lucky. There, white cats are the bringers of good

fortune and are encouraged to cross the paths of the superstitious. In Russia, grey cats are considered lucky, as they are in some parts of the United Kingdom.

In Ireland, black cats are believed to absorb their owner's pains, so if someone in the household is ill, their black cat is encouraged to stay in the sickroom. In parts of the United Kingdom it was thought that if a sick person was washed and the washing water was thrown over a cat, the illness would be transferred to the animal. It was once believed that if a cat left a household where there was illness (and who would blame it if it was doused with water!) the sick person would die. And it was an omen of worse health to come if a sick person saw two cats fighting, or dreamt of a cat.

Cats provided 'cures' for illnesses too. Anyone suffering from a stye on their eyelid was recommended to rub it with a black cat's tail – a tomcat's tail for a woman and the tail of a female cat for a man. Stroking a wart with the tail of a tortoiseshell cat would cure the wart – but only during May. Three drops of cat's blood would also cure warts but obtaining the blood probably ended in the person with the wart covered in blood – their own!

Cats have gained a superstitious reputation as weather forecasters. If a cat sneezes, rain is on the way. If a cat sneezes three times, the whole family will develop colds. If a cat washes over its ears with a paw, rain is due. If it runs about wildly it will turn windy and if it sits with its back to the fire there will be a storm.

Actors are very superstitious people so it isn't surprising that they have cat superstitions of their own. It is very lucky to have a cat living at the theatre but bad luck if it runs across the stage during a performance. However, a stagestruck cat would escape without punishment as it is considered very bad luck to kick a cat!

What do you call a cat who lives in a desert at Christmas time?

Sandy Claws.

Do cats like travelling? And what should I do with my cat when we move house?

Most cats don't like travelling at all and will let you know – noisily – during the entire journey that they would much rather be somewhere else. Making your cat as comfortable as possible is the only way to make the journey easier.

If travelling by car, your cat must be secured. If allowed to roam around loose, it could get under the driver's feet or under the pedals and cause an accident. Sometimes a cat which is used to wearing a harness and leash will sit on its owner's lap quite happily, held by its leash. Some cats prefer this method of travelling to the only alternative – a cat carrier.

Line the carrier with a comfortable sheet or blanket for the journey. If your cat is prone to travel-sickness, use newspaper as lining. Don't feed a cat which is a bad traveller just before a journey, but ensure it has water to drink.

Cardboard boxes do not make good carriers. Most cats

become frightened when they're not able to see what is going on and a frightened cat may rip its way out of a box. Or the cat, in fear, may urinate in the box, which causes the box to disintegrate and the cat then escapes.

Ask the driver to drive slowly and smoothly, especially around corners, so that your cat isn't tossed around in its carrier. If you are travelling for a long distance, bring water and a bowl for your cat, as well as a litter tray, and food, if necessary. If you leave the car, even if only for a few minutes, don't leave your cat inside on a hot day; it can lead to heat stroke, even death.

Many cats don't mind train journeys and may make less fuss than when travelling by car. Underground railways aren't a good idea though; most cats are frightened by the sudden noises and the rush of air.

If it is likely that you will have to take your cat on a long journey, or take it for regular journeys, you can accustom it to travelling by taking it out for very short trips and rewarding it with edible treats when you return. Then travelling becomes a pleasurable experience. If, however, you only take your cat in the car once a year for inoculations at the vets, you shouldn't be too surprised if your cat is unenthusiastic!

If you are moving house, several removal firms now have a pet removal service too and will take your cat (or dog, goldfish or gerbil) to your new home for you. If you're moving overseas there are specialist firms which will transport your pet and deal with all the paperwork involved.

If you are moving and dealing with your pet's removal yourself, it will be much less stressful for your cat if you:

- Lock your cat into an unused room (such as a bathroom) while the removal men are packing up. It should be

provided with a litter tray, food and water, and be left in peace and quiet until the removal men have gone.

- Place your cat in its secure carrier and take it to your new home.
- When you arrive at your new home, place your cat somewhere it won't be disturbed. The bathroom is probably the best place if no furniture has to be moved in there. Make sure there is no way it can escape and provide it with its tray, food and water.
- When the removal men have gone, check that windows and doors are closed and that fireplaces are blocked off (a frightened cat will hide anywhere dark and enclosed). Let your cat out of the bathroom and let it explore at its own pace. It will be nervous at first because cats are territorial and hate moving to somewhere new.
- Don't let your cat out of doors until it seems to be settling down. This will take at least a week. Some cats will take three or four weeks to settle down. When your cat is allowed out of doors, go with it and keep it company. There will probably be other cats in the neighbourhood who think *they* own your garden and will fight with your cat. Go outside with your cat, and chase away any other cats by shouting and waving your arms at them. (You may look silly but your cat will appreciate it.) Bring your cat in after ten minutes. After a few days of shouting and arm-waving, your cat may feel brave enough to face the neighbours' cats alone. However, by this time your new neighbours will probably think you are a little odd!

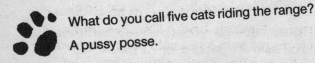

What do you call five cats riding the range?

A pussy posse.

Can I take my cat to a cat show?

You can show your cat at almost any cat show in the United Kingdom, whether it is a pedigree cat or a non-pedigree cat. The only cats which cannot be shown are non-pedigree adults which have not been neutered, female cats which are still nursing kittens, and kittens under three months of age. You must plan in advance as your entry must be received and accepted about a month before the show date. You can find out about shows by reading a cat magazine, or by looking in your local newspaper for details.

Only enter your cat for a show if you think it will enjoy it. Some cats love the fuss and attention they receive at a show; others hate it. The cats which hate shows will not win prizes if they growl at or bite the judges. If it's your first show, choose one which is near your home as this will be less stressful for your cat, especially if it doesn't like travelling.

Send the show manager a stamped, addressed envelope for your entry form and, when it arrives, fill it in carefully. All the rules you will need to know about the show will be sent with the entry form.

Cats are usually entered in one open class and several side classes. For a pedigree cat, the open class is its breed class – for example, Burmese, Siamese, British Shorthair. For a non-pedigree cat (referred to as household pets), the open class is its colour – for example, black, white, tabby. The

side classes may include special classes for cats which have not been shown before or for female kittens, or whatever. There may be some fun classes for non-pedigree cats to find 'the cat with the loveliest eyes' or 'the cat the judge would most like to take home'. Don't enter your cat for too many classes at its first show because, if it is not used to being handled by strangers, it may become bad-tempered.

Shows last all day, usually on a Saturday but sometimes on a Sunday. You will have to arrive early, before the public is allowed in, and you are not allowed to leave with your cat before the end of the show. So you will have to be at the show hall from around 9 a.m. to around 5.30 p.m. – maybe even a little longer. Your cat will spend that time in a pen and you will have to pay for the hire of the pen (sometimes called a benching fee) as well as paying for each class in which you enter. It will cost, on average, around £15 to enter a show, whatever sort of cat you have. If your cat wins, or comes second, third or fourth, it will receive rosettes. If it is very lucky, it might win a trophy, or some cat food from a sponsor. Sometimes 'specials' are given by individuals; these can be small trophies, books, cat ornaments or rosettes.

Before you and your cat are allowed into the show hall, your cat will have to be vetted-in. A vet will be there to check that your cat is healthy and has no fleas or other parasites. If your cat is unwell it will not be allowed to compete. You must also bring an up-to-date inoculation certificate to show to the vet. As you are vetted-in you may be given your tally, if this has not already been sent to you. A tally is a round label numbered with the number of your cat's pen. The tally should be tied around your cat's neck with a white ribbon. You will also be given a vetting-in card which you should display on your pen.

You will need quite a lot of equipment for a show. You

must have a secure cat carrier – you may be turned away if you turn up with your cat in a cardboard box. You'll also need a blanket for the bottom of the pen, a litter tray and food and water bowls. For some shows, all equipment (except carrier) must be white – your entry form will explain this. You'll also need to bring your cat's comb for any last-minute grooming and some tissues for tidying up.

Rules for judging vary according to which organisation is holding the show. At some you will have to leave the hall, or stand at the side while judging is carried out at each cat's pen. At others, the cats will be taken out of their pens to a judge at a table, who will comment on the cat publicly (this can be very embarrassing if your cat has grubby ears and the judge comments on it!).

Remember that you mustn't touch any cat but your own and you are perfectly entitled to ask people not to touch your cat. Touching can spread infection from cat to cat very easily. Many cat-lovers won't show their cats at all because of the risk of infection.

If you do decide to show your cat, preparations should begin months before the show date. Your cat should, of course, be receiving a good diet. A well-fed (not fat) cat will look healthy and a healthy cat is an attractive cat. You must brush your cat regularly. For the fortnight before the show, your cat should be brushed at least once a day. If a bath is necessary, bath your cat five days or so before the show. This allows time for the natural oils which may be washed out, to return to the coat. Ears should be spotlessly clean, as should claws, which should be neatly trimmed (see page 36).

Taking your cat to a show can be fun and it can be exciting if you win or depressing if you lose. Win or lose, as long as *you* know that *your* cat is the best cat in the world, that's all that matters. Good luck!

Moggy meanings

blue	what grey is called in the pedigree world
CA	Cat Association. An organisation similar to the GCCF, but newer. Its address is Westways, 26 Abbey Road, Medstead, Alton, Hants GU34 5PB. Telephone: 0420 62300
dam	a cat's mother
feline	a cat, or the cat family
GCCF	The Governing Council of the Cat Fancy. An organisation which registers pedigree cats and provides rules under which cat shows are held. Its address is 4–6 Penel Orlieu, Bridgwater, Somerset TA6 3PG. Telephone: 0278 427575
IPCS	Independent Pet Cat Society. This organisation holds shows specifically for non-pedigree cats and pet quality pedigree cats. Its address is 35 Coven Road, Brewood, Staffs ST19 9DF. Telephone: 0902 850567
kink	a malformation of the tail
kitten	in the United Kingdom, a kitten is nine months old or less. (In the USA it is ten months old or less.)
litter (1)	a group of kittens, usually born over a period of a few hours, to the same mother
litter (2)	the substance, used in litter trays, which is used as a toilet medium for cats
Longhair	the name given to all cats with long, fluffy fur
neutering	a veterinary operation on a male cat to prevent him fathering kittens
pedigree	the name given to a cat which has at least three generations of pure breeding
queen	female cat
red	what ginger is called in the pedigree world
Shorthair	the name given to all cats with short fur
sire	a cat's father
spaying	a veterinary operation on a female cat to prevent her having kittens
tomcat	a male cat